MIRACLES IN MY LIFE

MIRACLES IN MY LIFE

Testimonies of God's Blessings in My Life

BY
CAROLYN MCCORMICK

XULON PRESS

Xulon Press
2301 Lucien Way #415
Maitland, FL 32751
407.339.4217
www.xulonpress.com

Paperback ISBN-13: 978-1-6322-1343-3
Ebook ISBN-13: 978-1-6322-1344-0

TABLE OF CONTENTS

INTRODUCTION
GOD OF MIRACLES

God also bearing witness both with signs and wonders,

with various miracles, and gifts of the Holy Spirit, according to His own will.

(Hebrews 2:3 NKJV)

This book contains some of the many miracles God has performed in my life, yet I know the miracles have no end because the eternal life I have been given by the Lord Jesus is the greatest miracle of all! He gave me the faith to believe and receive Him as Savior and Lord. The miracles continue day by day and ultimately point to that greatest miracle of all, my heavenly home with the Lord forever. Perhaps by writing this book, I will be used of the Lord to encourage those who read it to be aware of the miracles God sends to them each day. My hope is that the readers will write down the account of their miracles so they can be an encouragement to their friends, families, and others who walk through the pages of their lives.

What is a miracle? Is a miracle a blessing? Is every blessing a miracle? The answer seems to be "yes" and "yes!" A miracle is something only God can do.

**One of the most intelligent men of all time once said,
"There are only two ways to live your life:
One way is as though nothing is a miracle.
And the other is as though everything is a miracle."
His name was Albert Einstein.**

I have always seen life itself and everything good in life as a miracle. Every breath is a miracle. As a Christian, I see my physical life as a miracle from God as you will understand as you read through the many miracles God sent to heal, protect, and provide for me throughout my life. My relationship with Him and His gift to me of eternal life are the most amazing miracles of all.

*Every good gift and every perfect gift is from above,
and comes down from the Father of lights,
with whom there is no variation or shadow of turning.*
(James 1:17 NKJV)

PART ONE
CHILDHOOD MIRACLES

Before I formed thee in the belly I knew thee;

*and before thou camest forth out of the womb I
sanctified thee*

(Jeremiah 1:5a KJV)

1

MY BIRTH

December 16, 1937

On a frosty December morning, I was born, Eddie Carolyn Owens, in Savannah, Georgia. My mother had painful labor for 72 hours due to a growth obstructing my access to the birth canal and was running a high fever. When the growth was finally discovered, she was taken into surgery and the growth was removed. A short time after the surgery Mother broke out with chicken pox. The medical personnel panicked! A short while later I was born, covered with chicken pox! We were told the chances for this condition was one in a million! As a precaution, Mother and I were put in quarantine. Tests were run to make sure we did not have smallpox. It was a tense situation, to say the least!

The fact that I had no permanent damage was also a miracle. My Mother had cravings during the pregnancy for the cubed starch she used for the family laundry. She ate the starch during the nine months she carried me.

The Lord was protecting me from danger right from the very beginning of my life.

- 2 -

THE BIRTH OF MY BROTHER

May 11, 1939

My brother, Alfred Franklin Owens, was born in Atlanta, Georgia. Mother had been warned against having more children after the problems she had during her first pregnancy and delivery, but she and Daddy wanted another child. "Buddy," my name for him since I could not say "Brother," was born seventeen months after my birth. Mother had blood poisoning during the nine months she carried him. Another growth had formed in her female organs during the pregnancy. Since the doctors were alerted to the possible problems she might have due to the previous pregnancy, they removed the growth and Buddy was born on Mother's Day weekend with no further complications.

God had a specific plan and purpose for both of our lives.
Jeremiah 29:11v

-*3*-

ASTHMA

As a small child, I had asthma so severely that my breathing was limited. One morning I started turning blue from lack of oxygen. These were the days before CPR was widely known and there was no 911 Emergency Service available. Mother and Daddy prayed for me as they sat at the kitchen table (James 5:15). As I lay in my bassinet near the table, they noticed my attention being directed to the grapefruit they were eating and thought I looked as though I wanted something to eat. Thinking it would not be harmful to give a few drops of the juice to me, they began feeding me little spoonful of the liquid. My breathing passages gradually opened and color returned to my face! They knew I would be all right! God had granted their request. The asthma attacks continued from time to time, but with less severity until I "outgrew" the condition at the age of twelve.

God was at work all the while, healing me in a gradual way.

Eye Injury

When Buddy was three and I was five, we were playing with stuffed toy bunny rabbits we had been given for Easter. He pulled at one of the bunny ears and the wire holding the ear in place came loose, piercing the pupil of his right eye. Infection set up and spread to the left eye by the time our parents got him to the doctor's office. The sight in both eyes was threatened. Mother and Daddy turned to the Lord in prayer on Buddy's behalf. The left eye was healed, having 20/20 vision restored, although the sight was gone in the right eye. As he grew up, he said he never thought of the loss of sight in the eye being a handicap since he could not remember seeing with both eyes.

Jesus answered, *"Neither this man nor his parents sinned, but that the works of God should be revealed in him."*
(John 9:3 NKJV)

POLIO

My daddy had polio which affected both his legs when he was three years old. He knew the limits the illness had caused through the years. He usually had to walk with a cane to steady his steps. His worst fear was that one day his children might have the disease. He watched me closely as I began to develop and was concerned when I showed very little interest in walking. Once I did start walking at about thirteen months of age, Daddy was relieved.

We were living in the Atlanta, Georgia, area when the polio epidemic was rampant. Buddy and I were together most of the time, yet he contracted the disease that weakened his legs, but miraculously, I was not stricken. Buddy was taken to Warm Springs Hospital in Georgia and given the Kenny treatment discovered by Sister Kenny. The treatment saved his right leg from muscle damage, though the muscles of his left leg could not be strengthened due to permanent damaged. The doctors told our parents that Buddy needed to stay at Warm Springs in the hospital for six months. He wore a brace from his hip to his ankle from age three and into manhood. He had to have the heel on his left shoes customized to allow the brace to be attached. One of Buddy's fondest memories is the Christmas he was given cowboy boots, thinking he could not have any kind of shoes other than the standard shoes. His good attitude toward his handicaps was an inspiration to others. Each year at the annual March of Dimes drive, Buddy and a friend Lavon, who also had polio, were asked to come to the center line during basketball tournaments as the appeal was made for funds.

**Buddy always said God had to slow him down
and used the handicaps as a blessing to help him grow
spiritually.**

Daddy was a great help to him in his adjustments since he had been through similar problems growing up with the physical limitations that polio presented. They enjoyed doing activities that did not require standing for long periods of time. Fishing was one of their favorite pastimes.

Daddy also taught Buddy and me to play the ukulele when he was six years old and I was seven. Later he taught Buddy to play the guitar as well. We spent many hours singing with Mother and Daddy at home as she played the piano and we played our guitars and ukuleles. This would remain one of my favorite memories and contributed to my love for singing harmony in duets, trios, quartets, ensembles, church choirs, college choir, and seminary touring choir through the years. Having no youth choir in our church, Buddy and I sang with our parents in the adult choir when we were in our teens until we enrolled in college. Being in a musical family brought us much joy and we learned to worship our God and thank Him for our miracles from an early age!

PRESIDENT FRANKLIN D. ROOSEVELT

My parents were told there were no private rooms for my brother at the Warm Springs Hospital due to the polio epidemic and the number of patients crowding the facility. Daddy was very upset by this and asked for an appointment to see President Roosevelt in order to seek his help in getting a private room away from the other polio victims. When Daddy realized he was actually going to have an opportunity to talk with the President of the United States, his hero, a fellow polio victim, he hardly knew what to say. My brother was named Franklin after the President. The President immediately put Daddy at ease as he asked Daddy what he could do for him.

My daddy told him he wanted to get a private room for his three-year-old son who had polio. The President agreed to arrange for a private room and asked if there was anything else he could do for Daddy. In humility, Daddy told the President he needed a job. The President asked him where we lived. Daddy told him we lived in Pembroke, Georgia, near Savannah. FDR made the necessary contacts for Daddy to get training with the Internal Revenue Service in Atlanta. Eventually, Daddy worked for IRS at the courthouse in Savannah, the job he held until he died in 1957. Daddy had only completed the eighth grade. My mother, who was in the upper 1 percent of her class and had taught in a one-room schoolhouse at age sixteen, taught my daddy his high school math. Daddy learned quickly and in 1954 he was number one in collection of taxable cases in the State of Georgia.

"For with God nothing will be impossible." (**Luke 1:37 NKJV**)

BUDDY'S INJURY

When Buddy was about six years old, he and I were swinging in our back yard. Buddy was holding a large stick in his hand. Mother told him it was dangerous and to put it down, but he decided to jump out of the swing and fly through the air still holding tightly to the stick. As he landed, the stick went into his mouth and down his throat. Mother rushed him to the doctor. There was damaged to his throat, but the doctor believed Buddy would recover with time. The wound healed slowly and Buddy had many difficulties eating and drinking. When he drank, fluids often came out his nose or he got strangled.

God protected him from what could have been a
life-threatening situation,
and he soon returned to his adventurous activities.

HIS HEALING TOUCH

When I was six years old, I had strep throat as well as appendicitis. I was in a lot of pain and ran a high fever of 105 degrees. My fever caused me to be delirious. I could see what appeared to me to be demons in the top corners of the room where I lay and felt the evil that frightened me. I remember my family praying for me. My daddy would sing to me as he played his guitar and then I felt better. The family doctor came to our home to examine me but indicated he could not take out the appendix or the tonsils due to the danger involved. He felt there was not much he could do for either condition.

God's touch healed me in His time.

-9-

SALVATION AT AGE NINE

My parents were Christians and had always attended church with my brother and me, but their closeness to God was not enough for me to be made right with Him. My own sin had to be dealt with and removed by Christ's death on the cross as payment of the debt I owed.

In my bedroom, I felt Christ's Spirit so strong I realized He was calling me to be His and to accept the gift of salvation He offered. I wanted Him to come into my life and be in charge. I agreed with Him that I was a sinner and He was the only Savior.

After telling my parents about the Lord saving me that day, I made a public profession at the Sunday worship service in April of 1947. I was baptized soon after to signify death to self and a new life in Christ. It was the most glorious experience I had ever known! I was afraid of being in deep water, but the night I was baptized, the Holy Spirit filled me with His peace. I felt clean and pure as my pastor took me under the warm water and presented me to the Father. Coming out of the water I knew the Spirit of God was upon me in a powerful way.

**After that night I wished everyone had the
experience that I had,
awakening the evangelistic spirit within me.**

-10-

THE FISH HOOK

Daddy and Buddy went fishing often. They would spend the night near the river bank in a little one-room cabin Daddy built out of scrap lumber. He placed a plaque over the screen door which read, "Cabin of Dreams." Daddy was a great fisherman with lots of patience and taught Buddy to be a great fisherman, too.

While on one of the fishing trips, Daddy got a rusty fish hook caught in his thumb. He and Buddy were miles from the nearest town and Daddy knew the fish hook needed to come out immediately. He told Buddy to get his pliers and pull the hook out of his thumb. Buddy was very upset and told Daddy he just couldn't do it. Daddy understood Buddy's reluctance to pull it out, so he took the plies and jerked out the metal hook himself, leaving a bleeding wound. He doctored the thumb the best he could with items from his First Aid Kit. Then he and Buddy prayed that the thumb would heal miraculously and there would be no infection.

As our family sat on the porch of our home four days later, Daddy told us the story of the accident and God's healing. He showed us his thumb. We could not see any sign of injury! The skin on his thumb was pink and smooth, just like the other parts of his hand. This remains one of my favorite miracles as God took special care of someone I loved with all my heart.

**Father God taught me much about miracles
through answered prayer that day.
It made me more aware of miracles in the years to come.**

- 11 -

MOTHER SPARED

As we were growing up, my mother washed our clothes in the bathtub because we did not have washing machine and hung the clothes outside to dry. One summer day, she took the clothes outside to pin them to the metal clothesline. As she walked back toward the house, lightning flashed out of the blue sky and struck the ground between the place where she was standing and the clothesline! She was just a few feet from the bolt.

**Perhaps evil forces planned to strike her that day,
but God's forces directed the bolt into the ground,
causing her no harm.**

ACCIDENT AT AGE TWELVE

Four days after my twelfth birthday, December 20, 1949, my mother was giving a church Christmas party. When she found out the pastor of the church was coming to the party, she asked me to go to the store about three blocks away and buy a gift for him. I road my bicycle to save time. On my way home from the store, I safely crossed the highway. As I peddled across the railroad tracks to the shoulder of the road, a car approached the 25 MPH zone going 85 MPH. When he saw the town appearing before him, he quickly applied the brakes, which pulled his car in my direction. After skidding over 200 feet, the car hit me and the impact threw the bicycle and me up in the air. Witnesses said I fell head first, hitting the windshield of the car with all of my weight bearing down on the right side of my head, and then fell to the pavement.

Back in those days, no helmets were worn when riding a bicycle. The bicycle was completely destroyed leaving me unconscious on the shoulder of the road. A man who worked in a car dealership nearby came running over to me and tried to find a pulse. Finding none and no breathing, he ran to our house nearby and told my mother I was dead.

"Not my little girl!" my mother declared as she stepped off our high porch and ran to me.

A man in the crowd that gathered had stopped by to see if he could help and was moving my arm back and forth, so by the time Mother knelt beside me I had shallow breathing, a weak pulse, and swelling on the right side of my head near my temple and eye.

My Daddy and brother had been gathering greenery and holly in the woods to decorate our house. As they drove by and saw cars gathered around the accident area, Daddy stopped to see if he could help the victim and saw it was me. The man who hit me was nearby and very frightened. He was a black stranger in a small Georgia town, driving a big shiny car. Daddy was very upset and confronted him as to whether he had been drinking alcohol. Fortunately for the man, he had not.

It took about two hours for the ambulance to arrive and I was finally taken to the hospital in Statesboro, Georgia, 25 miles away. By that time, the area around my right eye was bruised and swollen shut. The internal injuries included a fractured skull at the right temple and a brain concussion. About an hour after arriving at the hospital, I regained consciousness, seeing a bright light just before I awoke. Was I clinically dead as the man had told my mother? Was the light I saw coming from God's *she-kina* glory? Was I sent back from a heavenly state by the Lord? Only He knows.

It was a miracle of mercy that I survived that accident.

My entire family had been standing around my bed praying for me. I asked what had happened and where I was. My parents told me about the accident, but it was impossible for me to comprehend. In the days that followed I had several visitors. Among them was Prince H. Preston, Congressman from our district, who lived in Statesboro. He promised he would see that I had a great Christmas if I had to remain in the hospital.

I still did not know if I was going to die, but I had told God I was ready if He wanted to take me. I prayed my family would not be sad and lonely if God was going to take me to Heaven.

My Daddy came to visit during the day before going to work. I would tell him I was "fine." He would then relax, as he sat beside me, with his head resting on the side of my bed. Since he was not able to sleep at home because he was so worried about me, in a short time he would be asleep beside me. I had severe headaches and any movement or sound caused pain. The vibrations and sounds of his snoring were painful, but I would not wake him nor disturb his sleep.

The prognosis was that I would have headaches for approximately five years as the skull grew back pressing on a nerve. I could go home for Christmas, provided I stayed quietly in bed since I was still in a guarded condition. Bed rest was essential for two months, but I wanted to go back to school and keep up with my seventh-grade class work. So, after one month in bed, I attempted to go back to school. Though it was difficult, God gave me strength to make it through each day. Since He had saved me from death twice now from the day I was born, I knew He had more for me to do on this earth.

> *For You have possessed my reins: You have covered me in my mother's womb.*

(Psalm 139:13 Bible Paraphrase KJV)

Ask Yourself…

Are you aware of the miracles God sends to you each day?

How would you define a miracle?

Is a miracle a blessing?

Is every blessing a miracle?

Albert Einstein said, "There are only two ways to live your life: One way is as though nothing is a miracle. And the other is as though everything is a miracle."

Which way will you choose to live your life?

PART TWO
TEENAGE AND
COLLEGE MIRACLES

[I pray] the eyes of your understanding being enlightened,

that ye may know what is the hope of His calling.

(Ephesians 1:18 KJV)

GOD'S CALL

My brother and I went as visitors with the Pembroke Christian Church youth group to camp during the summers of 1949-1955 at Shellman Bluff near Glennville, Georgia. One night during our devotional time at Senior Camp, we were meeting in a prayer circle outside under the stars. I sensed a vision of God's spirit, a large form in the darkness like an angel, standing on my right telling me, in my spirit that He wanted me to serve Him in Christian work. It was an amazing personal experience, as though He came to speak directly to me.

There were no words, just the knowledge of what His spirit witnessed to my spirit
and I knew that I knew He was calling me to serve Him in a special way.

-74-

ACCIDENT ON THE MOUNTAIN

At Ridgecrest Baptist Assembly in North Carolina, as a part of a group of teenagers from our Baptist church in Georgia, I had another accident involving head trauma. Although I was only fifteen at the time, I was asked to be one of the chaperons for the group. That week at the conference I had made a further commitment to follow the Lord in a Christian vocation along with hundreds of youth from all over the United States. Our male chaperon had mentioned that my decision would mean college and seminary training and wondered how my family could afford it. Having a spiritual gift of faith, I could see no obstacles, financial or otherwise, if the Lord was leading me in that direction. God had called and would provide I told him! I only had to be willing and submissive.

One day during the retreat, our group joined others who were climbing Rattlesnake Mountain, considered one of the easier mountains to climb. While on the climb, a few of us in our group had stopped to rest at the foot of a huge boulder on the steep mountainside. A young boy on the edge of the knoll above us tripped and came falling down. He screamed for us to watch out, but I could see he was going to fall near the edge of the slope and possibly be killed. It was an automatic response as I reached up and caught him. His head hit mine on the right side where the injury had occurred three years prior from the car accident. The young boy slid out of my arms, receiving only a few skinned places on his side from the rocks, but he was safe.

Being temporarily blind and deaf, I realized I was awake but could not function fully. After a few minutes, I began to hear voices though it was as if they were far away. As my sight and hearing returned, I began to experience a great deal of pain. The headaches that resulted from the previous trauma were to continue four additional years due to the second head injury.

However, God had miraculously saved both the little boy and me.

– 15 –

GOD'S CONTINUED LEADERSHIP

At age seventeen in my senior year of high school, I prayed if God wanted me to go to college that He would send a representative to my high school to talk with me about the place He had chosen. Although our high school was the county seat school, we only had twenty in the senior class, so not many college representatives would seek students there. If a college representative came to my school, I would know it was God sending a miracle to me.

A few months later, Vice President John Womble of Bessie Tift College, Forsyth, Georgia, came to my school to talk with girls interested in Christian education. To my knowledge, I was the only student who signed up for a conference with him. I believe God had sent him just for me. He talked with me about a work scholarship that would help pay for some of my tuition. A college loan was also available that I could repay after I graduated.

In early September, my parents took me to enroll in Bessie Tift College. My daddy had tears in his eyes as he told me good-bye. I was so excited about going to the college God had chosen for me, yet I did not want to do anything that would make my daddy sad. I had mixed emotions as I hugged my parents and watched them drive away.

This was the beginning of four of the happiest years of my life. It was exactly where God wanted me to be to grow closer to Him during this formative period.

I had not read a brochure from BTC or seen the college before I enrolled.

God had assured me that this was the place where He was leading me.

-16-

1957 Tragedy

My Daddy and I could always talk openly about what was in our hearts. He listened to me and guided me in learning how to make decisions. He would ask me to think of three possible ways to work out any situation I was facing and then have me choose the one I thought would be best. Then he would support my decision. Usually, the first impression I had was the best choice. He was wise in the way he allowed me to make my own decisions and build up my confidence as I used the common sense the Lord gave me.

While I was home from college for the Christmas holidays in 1956, I realized Daddy was emotionally disquieted about the problems he faced. I reminded him God could take care of anything in his life, as he had taught me through the years. He said this time God could not help. This was not the "daddy" I had always known. I was greatly concerned about his depression. When I returned to Tift College after the winter vacation, I prayed each night for God's guidance.

As I prayed, I looked out the window toward the night sky. I noticed the pattern of the moonlight refracting through the screen appeared to be in the shape of a cross. God allowed me to see a vision of the events that were to happen when I would be informed about the great tragedy to enter my life concerning my Daddy. I prayed the Lord would hold me up and give me strength to cope as I felt I would be needed by my mother and brother.

After about two months of prayer, the day came while I was setting my table of eight in the dining hall for the supper meal. The Dean of Women, Ms. Flora Walraven, came to tell me the news concerning my Daddy's death. I could feel the form of someone behind me, holding me up as the sensation of a flowing robe, which felt like a soft breeze, swept across my legs. I noticed my arms come up in front of my body as though they were resting on the arms of a chair. Then I realized that the Lord was there, holding me up, as I had prayed. I knew in that moment, my Daddy was dead. I felt God's strength in my body and I relaxed in His arms. It seemed as though I floated up the two flights of stairs to the room where the college President, Dr. Carey Vinzant, was waiting for us.

As I sat down, I felt God's physical manifestation of His presence that had supported me, gently fade away. His peace and knowledge of what had happened remained with me. President Vinzant and Dean Walraven were silent, not knowing what to say. God helped me recall, once again, a time in our home a few months before, while having a family meal, when my Daddy had spoken about taking his life, but the Lord had helped him change his mind and come home to my mother, brother, and me. That was why I had prayed for two months to be prepared for Daddy's impending death. I knew it would happen.

"My Daddy is dead, isn't he? He shot himself, didn't he?"

Both Dr. Vinzant and Miss Walraven were overwhelmed with my knowledge of the details. I told her my Daddy had been depressed for a while and had talked about taking his life one night when I was home on summer vacation. I told the two college representatives about the first time I was aware of Daddy's suicidal thoughts and how God had prepared me for what was to come.

When I had packed to go back home, my friend, Mickey and other friends heard the news and came by my dorm room. She asked me to play my ukulele for her and sing one of our favorite songs. Mickey knew that it would be good for me to sing and play as I was waiting for my aunt to come take me home. Singing in the face of loss helped all of us deal with the tragedy of the day, a testimony of God's peace.

Once again God answered my prayer for Him to prepare me to be of help to Mother, Buddy, and others.

I experienced periods when I felt emotionally drained and would ask God to make me strong. I prayed constantly and praised God that my Daddy, who knew Him so well, was now with his Heavenly Father. As I viewed the body in the casket, I reminded my family, "Daddy isn't here. This is only the body as we knew him. He's home now."

Having my earthly father removed, I felt even closer to my Father in Heaven. I remembered the scripture in James 1:27 where God says He would "visit the fatherless and the widow" and I felt His special care. I was now a member of the special group called the "fatherless." God sent Carolyn, JoAnne, Johnny Faye, Marianne, Mary, Ruth and Sue, seven of my closest friends, to come from Tift College to my home the day of the funeral. It was a sacrifice of love and encouragement to my heart to see them walking in my front door! God continued to give me support through these special people in the weeks to come.

The strength God provided brought an unexplainable calm in my spirit. Months later when release was needed, He allowed the tears to come and helped wash away the hurt and loneliness that followed such a human loss.

**I had lost my best friend,
but I knew I had a Friend that would stick closer than
anyone could.
He would never leave me!**

-17-

VISIT IN DREAMS

The Lord allowed me to visit with my Daddy in a dream soon after his death. I could see him sitting with me at home on the front porch, having one of our "talks." He was seated in the chase lounge, a very low place for him to sit. During his life, it would have been too hard for him to get up from that position due to his fragile legs and balance issues, but in his new body he could sit there with no problems and be able to stand up anytime he wished. He explained that he came back to see me because he knew I would understand why he had to leave, although other family members would not be able to accept his "parting."

In another dream Daddy was talking to me, drinking his iced coffee, dressed in a Hawaiian shirt. He was skilled at playing the Hawaiian steel guitar and had always wanted to take a trip to Hawaii. I could see him pictured in a place of Paradise that I knew he would enjoy. He told me it was lovely and one day we would share it together.

VISION IN THE BALCONY

While singing in a concert on our Tift College Choir tour one night, I looked up in the balcony of the large church and saw a veiled curtain opening from the middle and my Daddy's face filled the area. He was smiling at me. Then I realized that he was getting to hear our choir for the first time. I poured out my songs for the Lord and my daddy. I was blessed once again with a visit from my best friend.

CLOSURE

For many years I had a reoccurring dream that Mother, Daddy, Buddy, and I were in a swiftly flowing river and at the time of the dreams, Daddy was the only one in the family who could swim. He was a strong swimmer, but as the waters began to sweep us up into the widening stream, he would first rescue Mother and then my brother. As he began to tire, I would tell him to let me go so he would be safe. Each time I dreamed that dream he would return to get me. After his death, I never had the dream again. At last, he was safe and so was I, but what a loss in my life.

For I will turn their mourning to joy,
Will comfort them
And make them rejoice rather than sorrow.
(Jeremiah 31:13)

Ask Yourself...

Read Jeremiah 29:11. Do you believe God has a plan and purpose for your life?

Have you asked God to give you direction so you can fulfill His plan His way?

Looking back at your life, can you see where God prepared you in advance for a situation or circumstance in your life?

Remember, God will use various ways to strengthen you when you must face a tragedy or crisis.

What is His promise in Deuteronomy 31:6 and Hebrews 13:5?

PART THREE
AFTER COLLEGE MIRACLES

-20-

FROM EAST TO WEST

After completing my college training in 1959, I applied for three jobs. One job was that of Youth Director in a church about 60 miles from my hometown. My mother wanted me to apply with the local school board to teach school and live at home with her. A representative from the American Red Cross had visited our college and talked with us about working as either recreation workers or social workers with patients in military hospitals. I prayed about what the Lord wanted me to do and asked Him to have only one agency accept my application and offer me a job. All three agencies offered me a job! I realized that God could use me in any of those positions and it seemed He was telling me just to choose.

Having the chance to travel interested me so after much soul searching, I accepted the job with American Red Cross. After two weeks training at Maxwell Air Force Base in Alabama, the fall of 1959, I flew from Savannah, Georgia to New Bern, North Carolina to begin work as a Hospital Approved Recreation Worker with American Red Cross. My first assignment was in the military hospital at Camp Lejeune on the North Carolina coast. I enjoyed planning and conducting hospital approved recreation and working with the military patients on the Orthopedic Wards assigned to me. I learned a great deal from the military doctors and other ARC workers who lived with us at the Bachelor Officers Quarters a few blocks from the hospital. ARC workers were required to have college degrees and were given the honorary rank of Second Lieutenant, therefore housed at the BOQ.

The lifestyle of most of this group was extremely different from the sheltered life in my Christian family and Christian college. This required adjustments on my part. One of the blessings was making a lifetime friend named Marilyn. My affections were vulnerable as I allowed myself to date a doctor who worked at the hospital and lived at the BOQ. He was not a believer in the Lord Jesus although he had a Catholic background. This was the wrong person for me and not in God's will. Yet, God used this situation to teach me much about myself and my need for a closer walk with Him. God worked out the situation that I was unwilling or unable to work out and saw that I was transferred six months later to a new job at the Navy hospital in Yokosuka, Japan.

He worked in mysterious ways to lead me away
"as far as the East is from the West" as the Bible states it.

My mother was very concerned about me going to work in Japan. She had heard that President Dwight Eisenhower was not allowed to go to Japan around that time because there was an international problem in the Far East. I assured her that the Japanese government would not see me as a threat in any way and I would be careful. Anytime I left the base at Yokosuka, I checked the information made available to employees of the military hospital. The pamphlets revealed "Condition Green" locations and we were asked to avoid those areas. Most of the time, those were areas where members of the Communist Party handed out propaganda to the passersby, targeting young people they met on the street. We were always cautioned not to cause an international incident.

When my friend Marilyn came to see me from Hawaii where she worked in a military hospital with ARC, she wanted to see all she could while in the country, including the government's Diet Building in Tokyo. I was not sure if that was wise, but we went through the lobby of the building, saw the many clocks on the wall showing the time in countries around the world, and had no confrontations nor did we cause an international incident. On a bus tour of the city, we went to a tea ceremony, saw the grounds of the Imperial Palace, and other sites.

I loved the work in the Navy hospital but missed my doctor-friend although I knew God had moved me away from him. One of the first things I saw that made me feel at home in the foreign country was a billboard out in a rice field showing the RCA dog listening to "the sound of his master's voice." Other signs that reminded me of home were the Singer Sewing Machine Company, advertisements for Coke Cola, and theaters showing advertisements for American movies.

WHILE IN JAPAN

While in Japan, I had wonderful experiences seeing the castle in Odawara when I traveled to Tokyo quite often on the train. I bought a third-class ticket, although the clerk at the train station encouraged me, as an American, to go first class and pay extra to guarantee a seat on the train. When I purchased my ticket for about one American dollar, I saved money so I would have funds to spend at the famous Takashimaya Department Store. What an amazing store that was! On each floor, there were ladies who cleaned the escalator railings wearing white gloves. They would welcome customers and list what items were on that particular floor. On top of the store was an amusement park with rides and refreshments for children and attendants to care for them while families enjoyed shopping.

The Chinese food in Kamakura was excellent, as was the pizzas at a restaurant in Tokyo. My bag of popcorn atop Tokyo Tower was shared unexpectedly with a crowd of Japanese students who flocked around me as I enjoyed a view of the city. The Silk Hotel was one of my favorite places to eat when I had a little extra money. My friend Marilyn was not in the mood for the local cuisine when we had lunch there and took a chance that she could order ham, black-eyed peas, and cornbread. I told her to order and see if it was available. Sure enough, she got her American meal just as she wanted. After her return to Hawaii, I was delighted to attend the Kabuki Theater and Kokusai (similar to the U.S. Radio City Music Hall presentations).

One of the most amazing things I did with my work associates was climb Mt. Fuji one weekend in July. I was told that the top of the mountain was covered in snow 10 months out of the year due to the altitude. The afternoon we arrived at the foot of the mountain, we rode horses to stations one and two. We stopped at station three for a meal of Soba noodles and drank some "Ocho" (hot green tea) at a little shop on the side of the mountain. Then we lay down to sleep on rice mats on the floor in groups of six or so beside other would-be-climbers. About 3 A.M. the guide woke us up and told us to begin the climb. One "out-house" was nearby, therefore, a long line formed to use the "facilities," not knowing when we would have another opportunity. Two ladies in the Navy I knew from the Yokosuka hospital started the climb with me but decided the effort was too much and turned back after a few hours. I continued on the upward path with strangers united in a common cause.

The climb took about 10 hours. The air was light as we reached the top of the mountain at 12,396 feet and I was laughing at anything I heard from fellow climbers. A young Air Force pilot noticed my gleeful state, asked when I eaten last and offered me an apple. He said at 13,000 feet pilots were required to use oxygen mask due to the altitude. He told me that after I ate the apple things would not seem so funny. He was right. We took pictures of the snow-covered crater and then made our descent. Going down the steep, volcanic-ash-covered slope was a bit dangerous, but I fell only once. The tennis shoes I wore were not adequate and were torn to shreds by the time I had made my decent. After the train ride back to the base in Yokosuka, I read in the newspaper that 17,000 people climbed the mountain that same weekend. Many of them were Japanese natives who made a pilgrimage to the mountain they worship. Although considered an extinct volcano, I was told that the Japanese (or Nipponese, as they call themselves) believe the volcano will one day erupt again.

One of the most exciting and dangerous things I experienced while in Japan was the thrill of riding through Tokyo in a taxi cab! It may sound like a casual event, but they were not called "kamikaze cab drivers" for nothing. My favorite place to go on weekends was the Fuji View Hotel in Hakone near one of the five lakes at the base of Mt. Fuji. Though my friends warned me not to eat the fresh fruit that was sold on the road due to the danger of getting Hepatitis, I ate it anyway. I told my friends that I had all my shots when I left the United States and assumed I would not get sick. While I was overseas, I read in the paper that Kim Novak, movie star in California, had Hepatitis.

I ate the fruit from the fruit stands in Japan and did not get sick.

-22-

THROUGH ALL MY TRAVEL GOD KEPT ME SAFE

Through all my travel God kept me safe and helped me with my directions so I would choose the right colored train to take me to and from the base where I lived. The burgundy trains went to the northern part of the country. The blue and gold trains went near the Navy base in Yokosuka. I memorized the colors and was impressed to the point that each time in my dreams of traveling through the country, I saw the blue and gold train taking me "home."

**If I had a problem while traveling,
God usually sent an American serviceman to my rescue.**

It seemed that as a young American lady, I was protected and assisted by other Americans even if it was, as on one occasion, just to pull me out of a train car. I was standing shoulder to shoulder with fifty or so other people and could not get out when the doors of the train opened at my stop. During a train stop, there was only a few seconds allowed to get out safely. When the bells stopped ringing, the doors slammed shut automatically. As the doors closed, the person trying to get off could get caught in the doors if he or she did not move quickly.

On one occasion, my ARC friend, Becky, and I went to the Inn at the Fuji Hakone Izu National Park for the weekend. She had been assigned to a hospital in Korea and was to leave the next week. One afternoon, we rented bicycles and rode around the

40

Lake Kawaguchi near the Inn in Hakone. We did not know how far it was around the lake until we returned, extremely tired and asked the hotel clerk. We were amazed to hear we had peddled 13 miles! Covered in dust from the unpaved roads, too tired to go to the dining room to eat, we took a bath, and ordered a meal to be delivered from room service.

The next day when we were ready to check out, we did not have enough money to pay the bill. We only needed a few yen. I told my friend that was no problem. There was a group of servicemen from Tachikawa Air Force Base in the same hotel and I knew they would loan us the money. When the men from the base came downstairs to pay their bill, I gave them my name, told them where I worked, and what we needed. One of the airmen said that he would loan me the money. I told him when I was paid I would take the train to Tachikawa, meet him on the base, and repay him. We went our separate ways. On payday, I took the train to the base, met him in the recreation hall, and paid him what I owed. I think he was surprised that I kept my word!

-*23*-

THE EARTHQUAKE

While working in Yokosuka, Japan, housing was provided for me by ARC in the quarters for military personnel and civilians who worked on the Navy Base. One night when I was sleeping soundly, I had a dream or so I thought. I could hear people running down the halls in the two-story building. It was very dark and I did not know what caused the panic. The next day at work, someone asked me if I got out of the building without any problems the night before. I did not know what they meant. They told me there had been an earthquake! My fellow workers could not believe I slept through it all! I told them about my "dream." They assured me that it was not a dream but a reality.

How glad I was that God took care of me and there was no damaged to the area where I slept so peacefully.

I slept much better before the movie "Psyco" came to Japan. I had to read the English subtitles on the screen since the audio was in Japanese. The theater was packed the night I went. None of my friends went with me. I am quite sure the shower scene has stuck in the minds of most people who saw the movie. Taking a shower after seeing the movie was a concern of mine because I shared a bathroom with a lady next door to my room. For the six months, I lived in the building, I never saw her. I could hear her going in the bathroom from time to time, but yet we never met.

God was watching over me even in these matters.

Ask Yourself...

Can you think of times when you know God must have been watching over you?

Do you recall times when God sent others to you when you needed help?

Record these events in a journal.

Read Psalm 37:23.

What is God's promise to you?

PART FOUR
RELATIONSHIP MIRACLES

-24-

FROM EMOTION TO DEVOTION

Within six months of working in Japan, my doctor-friend asked me to return to the United States and marry him. I resigned my job and flew to Boston, Massachusetts. In the fall of 1960, jet travel had just opened up from Japan to the Continental United States with flights on Wednesdays and Fridays. The day I left was the longest day I can remember, due to time zones in which I traveled. On Wednesday, November 30, 1960, I left Yokosuka, Japan at 3 P.M. I could see a big "Sayonara" ("good-bye") sign on the runway as the plane rolled by. I cried as I watched it disappear below as the plane climbed higher and higher in the sky. My emotions were stirred. I was leaving a wonderful place I had loved to share with friends, many of which were Japanese. I attended the base chapel and was one of the few Americans who sang in the choir with them. I also knew I would miss friends I had made in the hospital and on the ARC staff. But I wanted to be with the man I loved.

During the flight, we crossed the International Date Line and gained a day, the day I had lost six months prior when I went to Japan. On the trip over, I flew on Friday and lost Saturday completely. On the trip back to the States, we arrived in Hawaii during the early morning of Wednesday, November 30. I visited with Marilyn, my ARC friend from Jacksonville, FL. She met me at the airport during our layover, brought me a beautiful lea of fresh flowers to wear on the trip home, and gave me a brief ride around the island.

A few hours later I arrived in San Francisco, California. It was 1 P.M. Pacific Time. According to the clock, I had landed two hours before I left Japan! My friend, Nibby, a retired Navy Physical Therapist who had worked with me at the hospital in NC, met me at the airport. She asked me if I would like to go out and get a pizza for supper or what else would I like to do. I told her the only thing I wanted was for the next day to be the first day of December! Years later I saw the movie "Ground Hog Day" and was reminded of that long day, November 30, 1960, and my trip home from Japan.

The doctor-friend had moved back to his home in Boston, Massachusetts after his retirement from the Navy. During the time I was in Japan, he had begun working at Massachusetts General Hospital. After about a month spending time with him and visiting in his parent's home, I realized we were not going to get married. His family was Roman Catholic. He was short of statue, dark-skinned, and considered a Catholic. His Italian parents (primarily his mother) had concerns about his marriage to a tall blond who was a Baptist from the South. We were about as different as different could be.

He and I soon realized after talking things through, he was not willing to make the commitment of marriage and deal with all the religious, social, and cultural differences between us. We had a counseling session with a priest recommended by his mother. As we talked about our faith, the priest realized that the groom-to-be did not have faith in the Lord, but saw that I did. My doctor-friend realized I had given up everything to be with him, but he was not willing to give up anything for me. I felt betrayed and humiliated. My emotional desires controlled me at that point. I asked the Lord to take the situation out of my hands and help me deal with the fact that the marriage was not His will.

Two weeks later the Lord led me to return to my hometown in Georgia as I yielded to His control. Somehow, I had the faulty idea that if I went through with the marriage the Lord would work things out, touch the doctor's heart, and he would be saved. I realized as I prayed that I was just seeking my own desires and could not follow the Lord completely unless I let go of the emotional ties I had with this non-believer. I could not continue to hold onto the Lord with one hand and him with the other.

God wrapped His arms around me, forgave my sin, and let me know that my fellowship with Him had been restored as I accepted His will.

The Children's Home

I could not find a job when I returned to my hometown but was asked to type a thesis for a college student. We had a manual typewriter in those days, so the project took several weeks. I even had to use carbon paper to make copies. The lady paid me for typing the thesis, but I gleaned very little income from that project. My expenses were small since I was living at home with my Mother and the savings I had in the bank took care of my needs at that point.

As was suggested by the ARC representatives, workers going overseas were told to have half their salary checks sent to savings accounts, since the cost of living was so low at that time in Japan. I always saved a good portion of my salary anyway, so this was an easy decision for me. The savings were waiting for me in the bank as the Lord provided for my needs in advance.

He always goes before me and He makes the paths straight and smooths out the rough places. (Proverbs 3:6).

A friend contacted me a few months after I came home and told me about a job opening at the children's home 80 miles from Pembroke. My emotions needed time for healing. I prayed I would have a job that kept me so busy I would not have time to dwell on the pain of my mistakes. The Lord took me at my word as I became a Counselor and Recreation Worker at the South Georgia campus. I was on call 24 hours a day, having every third weekend off. My friend warned me that the leadership at the facility would not welcome the counseling aspect of the job and I would probably be asked to leave the position in a short period of time. Being a trusting person, I found this hard to believe. Time would prove his words to be an accurate prediction.

While working there, I asked God to help me find two ladies interested in singing in a trio with me. The daily routine at the facility was somewhat confining. I had never owned a car, so I had no personal transportation. To sing for the Lord was the best therapeutic outlet I could imagine and an opportunity for ministry. I was led to two ladies who were working at the Children's Home who had also been interested in doing some trio work but could not find an alto to join them. We began singing together at the country church across the road from the children's home. In addition to that opportunity, the baritone from the men's quartet at the church moved to another city and I was asked to sing in his place in that group. The pastor later asked me to be in charge of planning special music for the church services.

My prayer was answered three-fold. I learned to be careful about how specific I prayed. The Lord tends to answer me "word for word."

He directs the prayers, the very words I pray,
so He can bless me with marvelous answers.

-26-

THE FLAT TIRE

Periodically when the children needed medical or dental care, I was asked to take them to the children's home near Atlanta, GA. The children's home station wagon I was provided was in need of repair. Gas would leak out as we traveled, but we always arrived at our destination. One Sunday morning I was asked to take three teenage girls to a Baptist church about 100 miles away to be a part of the worship service. The girls sang two selections, gave testimonies, and shared information concerning funds needed at the home.

On the way back to the children's home, we started having a bumpy ride...an obvious flat tire! The girls panicked and wanted to know what we were going to do. I suggested that we get out and look both ways to see who the Lord was sending to help us. They were surprised at my faith but could do little about their situation. So, they began to watch and wait. In a few minutes, a car stopped. Three college students got out. One of them offered to help. The other two watched him change the tire as they flirted with the girls. We told them who we were, what we had been doing that day, and witnessed to them. One of the guys had been drinking but was on his best behavior when he found out we were Christians. With God's help, we made it back "home" in the old vehicle with adventurous stories to tell.

God gave us an opportunity to plant some seeds in the young men's lives and the girls had a chance to grow in their faith as they saw the Lord provide for our needs.

-27-

THE BRIGHT LIGHT

When I wanted to take a trip, I would borrow my mother's car, have it serviced, and return it after my trip. While driving back to South Georgia late one night from visiting my friend, Marilyn, who worked at Eglin Air Force Base in Pensacola, FL, I began to get sleepy. Normally, I do not have that problem when I am driving, but on this trip I needed help staying awake.

I prayed for the Lord to wake me up. Immediately following my short prayer, there was a bright ball of light that exploded in front of my windshield. It was about the size of a fist! There was no sound, just the silver bust of brightness!

I said aloud, "Thank you, Lord. I'm awake now!"

Just when I needed Him, He was there with the answer to my urgent prayer.

THE NAIL

On another occasion, I borrowed Mother's car to make a weekend trip to see a friend at Ft. Benning, GA. On Monday morning, I left early in order to arrive in South Georgia in time for work. After several hours of driving, I knew I had picked up a nail in my left front tire. Though it sounds strange, it was as though the Lord had let me know in advance what the specific problem was. I prayed that I could travel safely until I found a service station.

About two hours later, as the sun was rising, I came to a service station just opening for business. I told the owner of the business that I had picked up a nail in the left front tire. He could not believe that I had any way of knowing that. I told him the Lord had let me know.

The attendant checked out the tire and found a large nail still in the tire. The nail head had sealed in the air! God kept it inflated until I got to the station where the tire could be replaced! The attendant took off the punctured tire and sold me a retread tire for $7.50. I could not afford to buy a new tire and the spare did not have enough tread. Soon I was on my way and praying I would be back on the job in time for my work day.

**All things did work together for good and
my Father took care of every detail of my "going out
and coming in."**

-29-

TERMINATION

About 7 months after beginning the job at the children's home, Marilyn came to visit me for the day. After seeing that the softball games between the cottages was completed, I asked for and was given permission to leave the grounds by the director's wife. My responsibilities for the weekend had been fulfilled, so she saw no reason why I could not take some time off. I also asked permission to take two of the older teenage boys with us to Savannah for the afternoon to see a movie and do some shopping.

The director was out of town at the time, so his wife was the next person in the chain of command. I asked a fellow-worker to make sure all the recreation equipment was put back in the storage area. That night when I returned, the director had left word with the cottage parents who lived in the same cottage I did, that I had been fired.

Although I had been warned by the friend who recommended me for the job, I was still amazed when it happened! I spoke to the director the next morning. He told me I had not completed my work the day before because he had found "equipment" on the ball field. One of the workers told me a ball glove was found outside and the person I had asked to put up the equipment had failed to do so. The hardest part about the situation was telling the boys, who lived in the cottage where I lodged, ages 4-14, that the director wanted me to leave. I had gotten close to the children and they trusted me.

When I had moved in, one of them had asked, "Miss Owens, will you stay here forever?"

They needed to have the security of people around them who would give them love and always be "there" for them. Most of the 265 children at the Home had very little security in their lives. All but two of them had one or both parents living in either a mental institution or a penal institution. Many of them lived with the unrealistic hope that one day they would be united with their family and live happily ever after. Years later, I heard that one of the young ladies named Shirley, whose parents were deceased, realized her dream. She got married, left the facility, and provided a home for her brothers and sisters.

Since I did not have a way to get back to my home town the day I was relieved of my duties, Marilyn helped me pack my personal items and drove me back to Pembroke. For several months, I found myself home with my mother once again.

I had to deal with the emotions concerning inconsistencies in the leadership of the Christian organization and how they dealt with their employees. It was a trial of my faith the Lord used to help me mature in the work to which He was calling me. My experience in secular work with ARC had been more positive than my work in the Christian organization and that surprised me.

My ARC Field Director was an excellent supervisor who inspired me to improve in my work. She never spoke a discouraging word. I told someone I worked with in ARC that I would rather get a reprimand from her than a compliment from my immediate supervisor because of the director's gift of encouragement. The supervisor was discouraging. The Field Director was inspirational!

The Lord was teaching me how to depend on Him and not trust in man regardless of their labels. People do change and are sometimes inconsistent, but He never changes.

Ask Yourself...

Have I been seeking my own desires?

Have I been trying to hold onto the Lord with one hand and something I desire with the other?

Ask the Lord to help you deal with these issues. Record God's direction and guidance in your journal.

Read Matthew 6:33.

What is God's promise to you if you do what Jesus has instructed?

Part Five
Miracles in Atlanta

I began to pray for a job and felt the Lord leading me to work at the Home Mission Board in Atlanta, GA, or as I call it, the "Queen City of the South." I believe General Sherman must have left the plans to rebuild the city, however. You may agree with me if you have tried to drive in that city! When I moved to Atlanta, God provided me a room in the boarding house where Sue, a former college friend of mine, lived.

The first Wednesday night I was in town, I joined the choir at First Baptist Church. The following Sunday morning, I moved my membership at the end of the service to become a part of the body of Christ. The pastor, Dr. Roy McLain, "preached" a little sermon about the fact I was becoming a member of the church, wearing "an emblem of service" (a choir robe) and challenged the congregation to seek their place of service. What a wonderful experience being a part of that church! The large choir memorized all the music we used in the morning services each week. It was a challenge and a joy to be free to sing without stacks of books and folders to hinder us! The church staff became my second family as I got involved in all the opportunities offered me for service, including the singles' volleyball team where we competed with other church teams in the area!

In faith, I applied for a job at the Home Mission Board, knowing that was where the Lord wanted me to work. My friend, Sue, encouraged me to apply for a job in the business firm where she worked due to the good salaries and benefits. I applied at several business firms, but in my heart, I knew I would work at the Home Mission Board on Spring Street.

God gave me the assurance that He had a place for me in that agency.

At my interview with Dr. L.O. Griffith, Director of the Education and Promotion Division at the Home Mission Board, he was very gracious but explained there were no openings. I told him I understood, but I knew the Lord would open up a job for me. Having been taught to have faith, never doubt, and being given a spiritual gift of faith by the Lord, I had great confidence that I would be offered a job at the HMB in a matter of days. Dr. Griffith was amazed at my child-like faith! Two weeks later, he called to say that I had understood God's will and that the Lord did want me to work at the HMB. He said his department had needed someone for twenty-five years to assist Edna Simpson in Picture Service in the Education and Promotion Division and I was being hired!

I enjoyed the 15 months I worked with Edna and the other four people in that office. Dr. Griffith had started youth mission work in Kentucky years before coming to the HMB and I enjoyed hearing all his stories. I noticed most of the other workers did not have the same interest about his ventures in Appalachia. In order to hear the stories, I took an early bus to work at the HMB. That gave us time to share information about missions. My grandfathers had died when I was young child, so I did not remember them. Dr. Griffith filled that "grandfather" slot in my life and this allowed us to become close friends as well as co-workers.

While I was a member at First Baptist Church Atlanta, Cliff, the Minister of Music gave me many opportunities to sing in trios and with some of the leading soloist in the choir. I helped Joe, the Minister of Recreation, with musical programs for fellowships at the church and assisted him with the recreation program as a volunteer. We formed a strong friendship. I was close to all members of the staff and learned much about building a youth program from Jane, the Youth Director. Much of what she taught me helped me in the years to come when I worked as Youth Director in Southern Baptist churches.

Cliff gave me special opportunities to sing while I was a member at FBC. He chose me to sing with a professional group of ladies at the National Pork Convention held in an Atlanta hotel. Singers had to arrive by 5 A.M. The other ladies, friends of Cliff, had sung in the world of opera and were well known in classical music circles. As we were eating breakfast, the ladies asked where I sang.

They appeared unimpressed when I answered, "First Baptist Church Choir, in Atlanta and prior to that in the Tift College Choir and Ensemble."

The famous comedian, Sam Levenson, was the speaker for the morning. It was exciting for me to be there, even if the text of the classic operetta concerned sausages, both links, and patties! When Cliff presented me with a check, I was surprised it was within a few dollars of my Home Mission Board weekly salary, an unexpected financial blessing!

-30-

WRECK AT THE RESTAURANT

I moved into a boarding house in Atlanta to better fit my expenses on my $60.00-a-week income. I put most of my money in a saving account, a small amount in checking, and kept out about $10.00 in cash for "emergencies." A friend told me I must be expecting only small emergencies. That was the plan.

The boarding house was owned by a lady from North Georgia who bought the house to provide her young adult friends an affordable living place in Atlanta. The young people who lived there were eighteen to twenty years old and had grown up near the lady's home town. I was the "old lady" of the group at twenty-five years old. Our lifestyles were as different as night and day. It took some adjustments for me to get used to their preference in music and social activities. However, most of my time was spent at work at the Home Mission Board on Spring Street or at First Baptist Church on Peachtree North East.

The main reason for moving to this location was that it was only about six blocks to the church, well within walking distance, and near the bus stop. My church friends often insisted on providing me a ride to and from church services and activities.

The young boarders headed for their homes on the weekends which left me alone with the landlady. She would return to her "roots" from time to time. Since the other boarders were getting home cooking on weekends and I had to buy my food to cook in her kitchen or go out to eat at a restaurant, she decided she would take me out to eat on weekends when she was in Atlanta. That was a very nice "extra" for me. The lady was a bit high strung and her speech was rough at times, but she was thoughtful to provide for me on the weekends.

One Friday night, she told me we were going out for a seafood supper at one of her favorite restaurants. Edna, my co-worker from the Home Mission Board, had given me two tickets for the Atlanta Symphony concert for that night. I had asked my choir–member–friend, Faye, to go to the symphony with me. She planned to drive her car and meet me at the boarding house when I returned to my residence.

After the landlady and I ate our meal and prepared to leave the parking lot, she pulled out too far in the right lane of traffic. The front left corner of her car was hit by an oncoming vehicle. Her car was thrown forward and to the right, back into the parking lot of the restaurant. A witness told the police when they arrived that if the car had not zigzagged, it would have hit a large metal mailbox on the passenger side and I would have probably been killed.

I know the Lord sent an angel to guide the car away from the point of danger.

The impact threw me toward the floorboard of the car and my head landed in the driver's lap, the only safe place available! When I got out of the car, one of my new shoes was missing. It was later found on the floorboard of the car.

I called Faye to let her know about the accident. She arrived a short time later. Being a nurse, she was concerned about possible injuries I might have. She asked why I was rubbing my right elbow and wanted to know if I was in pain. I was not aware I was rubbing it or that it hurt.

All I could say was, "I can't believe my shoe came off. The shoes were so tight."

She told me she was not interested in my shoe, but wanted to know about my elbow. Evidently, I had bumped the elbow on the door, but I was not injured. The landlady was highly excited, talking loudly, and amazed we had not hit the mailbox or been harmed in any way. My friend was concerned about me, but since I thought I was all right, we continued with our plans and attended the concert.

God was there, through it all, protecting us as He promises He will.

God slumbers not nor sleeps, but keeps watch over His own. He is the ultimate promise keeper. "His eye is on the sparrow and I know He watches me." This is my song of testimony. Matthew 10:29-31 tells us that even when the sparrows fall, the Father takes note of His little creatures. He considers us of more value than many sparrows. Luke 12:6-7 reminds us God even numbers the hairs of our head. Some people ask and wonder if He really cares, but I know that He cares for and watches over me, day and night, for His own good pleasure.

-31-

BREAK-IN ATTEMPT

One weekend when the other boarders and the landlady had gone home for the weekend, I was home alone. Saturday night I had gone out with some friends for supper. After being home about an hour, I heard a noise on the front porch that sounded like someone walking. The land lady's Chihuahua began to bark with all his might! That brought me no comfort. If someone was on the porch, he would recognize the sound of a small dog barking and chances were he would not be frightened away. The dog tried to be brave and warn me, but at the same time was a bundle of nerves, shaking all over. I put little fellow in the back bedroom with me and prayed that the Lord would protect us. There was no phone in that part of the house, so the best thing I could do was rely on the Lord as I always did.

As a man tried to enter the front door, the landlady returned from out of town. She drove in the driveway in time to see a large man standing there. She began yelling and screaming uncontrollably! When he heard the shrill sound in the night, he darted off the porch and down the street. The landlady was still yelling when she came in the house, calling my name, asking if I was all right. I don't know who was happier to see her, me or her dog. For weeks before this event, we had been having problems with someone stealing our clothes off the outside clothesline, but no one had tried to break in the house.

**Again, the shadow of the Almighty rested over us
and we were safe.**

-32-

KNIFE SALESMAN

A neighbor advertised a house for rent that was closer to the First Baptist Church, so two of my friends from the boarding house and I moved up the street and set up housekeeping. Most of the time the girls went home on the weekends and I was there alone.

One warm sunny afternoon, a knife salesman came to the rental house where we lived. He asked if he could show me his wares. It could have been a dangerous situation for me. I observed in my spirit the way he relished talking about the quality and sharpness of the knives, almost in an obsessive manner. The Lord helped me be bold enough to tell him I was not interested in buying the knives and ushered him out the door.

After he left, I became weak when I thought through the time I had spent alone with him. Why I had the experience, I do not know. Why I allowed him to show me his wares and put myself in a vulnerable position, I do not know. Again, I felt forces in the heavens wrestling about me.

God's protection and wisdom filled my spirit. I was kept safe in Him.

Ask Yourself…

Has God ever given me the assurance that He had a blessing for me that others have doubted?

Have I ever wondered if God really cares for me?

Why did I feel that way?

How did He show me He cared for me?

Record these events in your journal and the insights you have gained from them.

Read Matthew 10:29-31.

What is God's promise to you?

PART SIX
SEMINARY CALL

-*33*-

SEMINARY CALL 1963

God assured me the time was right for me to enter seminary. Although I was told by a worker at the HMB that it was too late to be accepted for the Fall Semester, I mailed in my application to Southwestern Baptist Theological Seminary, was accepted, and enrolled in September 1963. While at seminary, I gave myself to the Lord to be used as a single person in His service, if that was His will for me. I had made a mistake choosing the wrong person seven years before and wanted God to do the choosing from that day forward. I wanted Him to be totally responsible for sending me a marriage partner if He wanted me to get married. As Abraham was willing to give up Isaac, I put marriage and children on the altar. The Lord was pleased as I passed the test and did not require that sacrifice.

God chose to bless me with that which I was willing to give up for His sake. He was ready to send David McCormick from Jacksonville, FL into my life. He was a first-year music student at SWBTS while I was entering my second year in the School of Religious Education. Billie Sue, a former Norman Park College friend of his and also a seminary friend of mine, heard David was coming to Southwestern Seminary in the fall and asked if she could ride out to Texas with him as summer break came to an end. The friend we planned to ride with that semester had a conflict in his work schedule and could not provide transportation for us. However, Billie Sue failed to tell David I would be traveling with them also.

My Mother took me to Albany, GA to spend the night with Billie Sue, the night before David was to stop by to provide a ride for "her." The next morning, I got up and was dressed before our friend, so when David rang the doorbell, I invited him to come in. We visited a bit while waiting for her to get ready. When David found out he was to provide a space for two of us to travel with him, plus our luggage, he told us he did not have room for one more sheet of music in his Valiant! Billie Sue's daddy said that was no problem since he was an expert packer. He took everything out of David's car and repacked it. With the use of his luggage rack for the suitcases on top of the car, he was able to find a place for all our things and room for us to sit in the front seat. We got very well acquainted in those close quarters on that long trip from Georgia to Texas. The most exciting event happened when we slowed down for traffic and a car behind us did not stop in time to avoid the impact with the Valiant's bumper. No one was hurt and the damage to the car was minor.

God's watch care was evident.

-34-

SUMMER YOUTH WORK

God led me to a summer job as Youth Director in Houston, Texas after my first two semesters at seminary. A psychologist from the church interviewed me at the seminary campus and recommended me to the committee at the church in Houston. I was called by a unanimous vote.

While on the church staff, I learned more about my calling to do church-related work. I was asked to start a youth program in a church of over 3,000 members. This job gave me a taste of working on a church staff and how to be a team member in ministry. The pastor had one meeting with me and informed me at that time that he was not in favor of the program, my being there on staff, and did not plan to be involved. He said the personnel committee had suggested a salary of $100.00 a week but he made sure that was cut to $80.00. He also told me I had no budget to use in the youth program! I was amazed that he did not plan to support the summer ministry but God gave me an answer. I told the pastor I preferred him being a part of the youth program, but if he did not choose to do so, the Lord and I would get the job done! As it turned out, I was able to have everything needed donated by parents of the youth and other church members, even equipment and $30.00 that was charged for Christian movies shown at our youth retreat.

There were two Sunday morning services each week, one Wednesday night, and one Sunday night. After the first week or so, the part-time Minister of Music told me the youth announcements were not being made in the early service. I began attending both services and made the announcements myself.

A couple in the church provided me a room in their home for the summer and a car to use for youth trips and my general transportation needs. Cliff, the man of the house, considered me to be a special missionary to their church and was interested in everything we did in the youth program. He, his wife, and two children were so gracious and made me feel at home during that summer I lived there.

The youth of the church responded beautifully to the program God helped me plan after I had prayed two weeks for His leadership and direction.

The Youth Council I felt led to organize worked with me effectively and we saw God accomplish great things in the life of the families in the church. I worked through the YC to involve the pastor, having the youth ask him to lead weekly Bible studies in their homes. The extra blessing was that he actually got to know the youth personally. He did not think they would be interested in spiritual things, but they matured in many ways during those three months and were eager to respond to the Lord.

Through recreational activities, Sunday night fellowships, youth retreats at a nearby camp, Bible studies, and drama club, the youth grew spiritually throughout the summer. The pastor was amazed that the Tuesday Night Bible study had the largest attendance of any weekly youth activities! Several of the youth witnessed to their friends at school and brought them to church fellowships. They became excited about their walk with the Lord!

The youth enjoyed taking me out to the area where the Astrodome was being built. It was interesting to see the stages of its development over the summer. A family in the church included me in their boat outings on Galveston Bay to grill steak and watch the sunset. The parents of the youth I worked with were very supportive.

-35-

MORMON TABERNACLE CHOIR TICKETS

One of the high points of the summer was getting to hear the Mormon Tabernacle Choir when they came to Houston on tour. No, they did not bring the organ! Members of the church had bought advance tickets. The night of the concert I found out the group was going to hear the choir. There was no time to get a ticket. I asked if I could ride downtown with them and take a chance that a ticket had been turned in by someone who could not attend. The group was amazed that I had faith to believe I would possibly get a ticket for the sold-out event the night of the concert! I told them if I could not get in, I would call Cliff, who worked downtown, and ride home with him.

I had nothing to lose and knew all things were possible.

When our church group started into the concert hall, I asked a policeman on duty near the entrance if he knew of any tickets that had been turned in that I could buy. He offered me four tickets. I told him I only needed one. He said I could just have the ticket and suggested I keep moving. I accepted the free ticket God provided, got a seat with my friends, and was blessed to hear the thrilling concert of Christian music! Throughout the concert, friends in our group would look at me and shake their heads, finding it hard to believe that I got in free!

Ask Yourself...

Have I fully given myself to the Lord to be used in His service?

Have I made a mistake choosing the wrong person in a relationship instead of asking God to do the choosing?

Record your prayer in your journal as you surrender your relationships to God and ask Him to choose for you from this day forward.

Read Psalm 143:10 and 1 John 5:14-15.

What is God's promise to you if you choose to seek His will?

Part Seven
Marriage and
Children Miracles

-36-

GOD PROVIDES A MATE

There were three times David and I could have met but in God's perfect timing, He kept us apart until He had us ready to meet each other. Through the years, we talked about these amazing circumstances and stood in awe at how God brought us together! David told me about a time he was in downtown Jacksonville on his lunch break when a large building was burning. He worked near the building and had come out to see the tragic site along with scores of other curious people. I was visiting a good friend in the city and we were downtown shopping on the same day when the fire destroyed the building. I remember the look on his face when I told him, "I was there that day!" David and I were on opposite sides of the street, just a few yards apart, and yet we did not meet.

During the time I lived in Atlanta and worked at the Home Mission Board, I was contacted by Rev. Roebuck from Rome, GA and asked to consider working on their church staff as Youth Director. The pastor came to Atlanta to talk with me first and then set up a date to meet with the Youth Search Committee at the church in Rome. I had been to Rome many times during my college days. Several of my good friends from Tift College were from Rome and my best friend, Carolyn, often took me home with her for the weekend. There were more ways to get to Rome than rides going to Pembroke, so I was in Rome often.

I met with the committee for a question and answer session. They took me out to eat and provided me a place to stay in the new Holiday Inn motel. The motel was opening the same weekend

I was being interviewed. Everything was complete except the landscaping and the parking lot. David and one of his good friends who were attending Shorter College were riding around on that Saturday and drove by to see the Holiday Inn. I was inside in my room. He was riding by the motel. Years later, we realized that if I had accepted the job offer I would have been his Youth Director since he was a member of the same church offering me the job. I would have worked with College and High School students. Chances are we would never have dated on that basis.

It was not God's time for us to meet.

David dated a few girls after getting settled at the seminary, but he and I were together every day. Our official dating started after months of being best friends, eating out almost every night, going to church together on Wednesdays and Sundays, singing in the church choir, and growing in our love. We knew God was leading us together and David told me on the first date on Valentine's Day 1965, that he knew we would be married. He spoke with such certainty. I was amazed! If that was what God wanted I was willing to consider the possibility but did not want to make a mistake due to my past experience. A group of ladies from the HMB had given me a shower before I left for seminary. One of the unmarried employees who brought me a steam iron said to me, "I hope you get some shirts to iron."

One day when David was stressed out with his work schedule, class load, and laundry chores, I said to him, "Maybe I could help. Let me iron your shirts for you." He was so pleased that I was willing to help him. As I was ironing the shirts, I remembered what the lady had told me.

Sure enough, God gave me shirts to iron and an opportunity to be a helpmate to David through years of marriage and ministry that followed.

-37-

MINISTRY IN NEW MEXICO

In the summer of 1965, I was far away from David, working in Las Cruces, New Mexico, at First Baptist Church as Youth Director. He was in Ft. Worth serving a small church as their Minister of Music. We learned that the longer you talked on the telephone the cheaper the bill. When you are in love you can make yourself believe anything, I suppose. We watched the Andy Williams Show while talking on the phone and listened to him sing some of our favorite songs, our special song being "Dear Heart."

After the experience with the pastor in Houston, I was pleased to have a cooperative church leader with whom to work in Las Cruces, New Mexico. Due to his last name being "Mormon," he got a lot of kidding from Baptists leaders in the New Mexico Baptist Convention. The entire staff in Las Cruces was supportive of the work I was called to do. The teen and college-age students were enthusiastic about the youth program and worked together with me to accomplish goals set by the Youth Council. I learned to love them and enjoyed life in the desert. It had its own special beauty. "From the mountains to the prairie" took on new meaning after the summer when I would sing "God Bless America."

Occasionally, I had a chance to do a little sightseeing at White Sands, New Mexico Space Center and Billy the Kid's hideout which had been converted into a restaurant called La Posta. The youth liked to take me across the border into Juarez, Mexico, for what they called a "youth trip," when they just wanted an excuse to go to Juarez. Crossing the border, I felt like I was in another world, stepping into the Mexican economy and seeing poverty so close to the United States border. I remember the cost of the large steaks we ate at a restaurant was about $1.00! I was told not to questions from "whence it came."

The most wonderful part of the summer was seeing many youth and adults dedicate themselves to the Lord. One man who had been an alcoholic for years was won to the Lord. His daughter and I prayed for him all summer. It was a miracle to see him attend church one Sunday morning and at the end of the service, respond to the altar call, giving his life to Jesus.

Nothing is impossible with God! How great it is to have a part in God's eternal plan.

GRADUATION AND MARRIAGE– MRE AND MRS

In January 1966, I graduated from seminary with a Master's Degree in Religious Education and in July of the same year David graduated with a Bachelor's degree in Church Music. In August of that year, we were married in Pembroke, Georgia. Reverend John Joyner, who united us in marriage, had also baptized me in the same church, First Baptist Church, almost twenty years before.

After a honeymoon in the Bahamas, we returned to Ft. Worth, Texas where I secured a job as teacher aide in a first-grade class. After a year, I applied for a job as bookkeeper at the Baptist Book Store on the seminary campus. The store was in walking distance of the four room apartment we rented from Dr. T.B. Maston, seminary Ethics Professor. I worked at the book store, posting accounts and working on the sales floor. The job allowed me a chance to get to know many students and professors. David worked in the Ft. Worth Public Library system, advancing to Assistant Librarian in a few months, finding favor with the Librarian due to doing a good job, even though he did not have a library degree.

-39-

LIGHTNING STRIKE

While we were visiting my mother in Georgia one weekend, clouds began to roll in and it looked like we might have some rain. I remembered a window in our car was down and decided to roll it up so the car seat would not get wet in case it did rain. The car was parked by a large tree in front of the sidewalk that led up to the house. I rolled up the window and walked back to the porch. As I reached for the door, lightning struck the tree next to the car where I had just been standing. The hair on my arms stood up from the implosion in the air. It was a very close call!

**I could have been killed, but God's angels were all
around me that day
and He gave me another testimony to write in
my book of miracles.**

THE MANSION ON THE HILL TOP

Dr. A. Donald Bell, seminary professor, came by the Baptist Book Store at Southwestern Baptist Theological Seminary one day before he left on sabbatical leave to go to the Philippines. He told us he planned to pay a caretaker $300.00 a month to watch over his house and belongings while he was away. Seeing the possibility of better housing and a chance of a lifetime to live in his beautiful house, I told him David and I might consider house-sitting for him for the same rent we paid our landlord, Dr. Maston, the amount of $40.00 a month. Dr. Bell was independently wealthy and did not need the money, but thought it was a quaint idea. He told me he would set up a meeting for David and me with his wife and discuss the matter. We met the couple later that week in their lovely three-story home. It was filled with antiques, some dating back to the thirteenth century. The couple decided to ask $45.00 a month rent for the year they would be gone.

It was amazing to live in the exclusive area of the city in a mansion that was next door to Ben Hogan's brother. Mr. Hogan was in an office supply business and must have been very busy. We never saw him the year we were there. The famous Ft. Worth golf course, where tournaments were held, was across the street from Dr. Bell's house, but we knew nothing about golf. We were surprised when people would drive up and ask if they could have permission to park in our yard during tournament week.

Sitting on the back deck of the house, we had a beautiful view of the Texas Christian University football field. One afternoon while going for a walk, we had to stop as we got close to the entrance to the university because a motorcade was pulling into the TCU stadium area. Seeing the decal on the limousine, and the US flag, we realized it was President Lyndon Johnson and his entourage! He was in town to speak at graduation.

First Child's Birth

A few months after we moved in the house, I became pregnant. Five months later, I had to resign from the Book Store due to the Sunday School Board policy concerning employees who were pregnant. After a perfect pregnancy at age thirty, I gave birth to Michele Lorayne McCormick on July 3, 1968. God blessed me through all nine months I carried her. The only problem I had was a bout with the flu in the third month. I had a problem free delivery, lasting only 7 1/2 hours after my doctor induced labor. He agreed to induce labor because David had been called as Minister of Music to First Baptist Church in Lake City, FL, and the doctor realized we were supposed to move in three weeks. He said he normally did not induce labor unless it was for an "important reason like the end of the year for tax purposes." That was an interesting perspective.

Michele was a beautiful baby with a good appetite and a strong body. She was born a week before the Bell family arrived back in the USA. It was a busy time, full of good memories and confusion also. Flowers were being sent to congratulate us on the arrival of our baby girl and baskets of flowers were being delivered to our address to welcome the Bells back home. The house looked like a florist shop full of baskets of roses, chrysanthemums, daisies, and other lovely flowers and gifts.

-42-

ANGEL UNAWARE

While cleaning the house one day, the doorbell rang. Although it was a hot summer day, the man at the door was wearing a heavy coat. He was a bit stooped and had on a gray hat. He asked if he could do some yard work to earn money. I did not have any work for him but assumed he was in need of food. I asked him to wait at the door and I went to the kitchen to see what I had to share with him. We did not have much in the cabinets, but I filled a paper bag with half of what was on my shelves. When I offered him the groceries, he thanked me and turned to leave. I was drawn to him by his penetrating eyes that seem to reach into my soul!

As he left, I closed the door and started back to the kitchen. Feeling the need to see him one more time, I went to the window and looked down the street to the right and the left. No one was there. I opened the door and walked out to get a better look, but still could see no one. I believe I had entertained an angel unaware. How blessed I was when I realized I had divided what I had with someone sent by God whom I would probably never see again.

God sent the experience for His glory and to inspire me.

THE BABY BED

In August 1968, we moved from Ft. Worth, TX to Lake City, FL where David had been called to become the Minister of Music and Youth at First Baptist Church. We were willing to go anywhere the Lord directed us and had prayed for His leadership. God sent us to the home church of David's grandparents, the church where he had visited as a child. The nursery worker at the church assigned Michele to a baby bed that had been donated years before by her great grandparents. The nursery worker did not know there was any relation since the last name was different from ours. The plaque on the baby bed read, "Donated by Mr. & Mrs. Willie Carl Harrison," parents of David's mother. When we read the plaque, we were amazed that the bed the relatives gave was selected for Michele's use.

God had used family members to provide for Michele years before we came to be members of the church.

—44—

BIRTH OF SECOND CHILD

Our second child was born on August 15, 1970, at the community hospital in Ducktown, Tennessee, a few miles from McCaysville, Georgia, where David had been called to serve as Minister of Music and Youth at First Baptist Church in my seventh month of pregnancy. Michael Shannon McCormick arrived after my nine months of good health and a perfect delivery lasting only four hours. "Daddy" was present in the delivery room for this occasion, whereas in Ft. Worth the father was not allowed in the birthing area.

Michael had an allergy to Enfamil formula, but that cleared up after four months. He was a low maintenance, good-natured baby, sleeping much of the time. In 1972, he developed asthmatic bronchitis just before his third birthday.

David was called to First Baptist Church in Buford, Georgia, as Minister of Music and Youth when Michael was two years old and Michele was age four. We bought our first house with help from a wealthy lady in that church who gave us $5,000 to help with the down payment. She was diagnosed with terminal cancer but continued to be faithful to meet needs. When we were looking for a home David was concerned that we could not afford a house. We were told rentals in the area were not "desirable." I had told David if the Lord wanted us to have a house, He would provide the funds.

**God blessed my statement of faith and
literally gave us the money.
We repaid her estate after she died two years later.**

Sing the Clouds Away

One summer, David and I taught at the Youth Music Camp at the Georgia Baptist Assembly in Toccoa, GA. He was to teach Theory and I was asked to teach the History of Hymns. Michele was about three years old at the time and Michael was a year old. We asked the leaders on staff for the ten-day conference if a nursery was provided and were told there was so we brought the children with us. After the rooms were assigned and we registered at the office, I asked about the hours when the nursery was open and was told there was a nursery from 10:00 until 12:00 on Sunday morning. This was of great concern to me because there was no one to watch the children when David and I would be teaching classes for the week. The Lord worked it out for us and some of the youth and other teachers on the staff and our Association Missionary shared times for babysitting.

During the week, the youth memorized the choral music and orchestral music in preparation for the production of a recording at the end of the week. When they were rehearsing, I took the children to our room so they would not distract the youth in the choral choir, the leaders and directors, the orchestra members, and handbell choir as did other parents with children at the assembly. On the day of the recording, all persons with children, not involved in the recording, were asked to stay out of the building, so that there was no chance of the children making noise or causing any problem.

I took Michele and Michael for a walk on the grounds. When we got to the lake area, we sat on the dock and looked at all the beautiful things around us. While we were sitting there, a dark cloud was being driven by the wind toward the lake. The children were concerned that it might rain. We felt a few sprinkles. I told them the Lord knew we could not go back inside. The doors to the assembly were locked after we left. I told the children that God would drive the clouds away. To teach them to rely on Him at all times, and increase their faith, I taught them a little song I had learned as a child. I don't know who wrote the words or music, but it was a favorite of mine. We began to sing.

"Sing the clouds away, night will turn to day, if we sing and sing and sing, we'll sing the clouds away. Smile to clouds away, night will turn to day, if we smile and smile and smile, we'll smile the clouds away. Pray the clouds away, night will turn to day, if we pray and pray and pray, we'll pray the clouds away. (Chorus) Sing and smile and pray, that's the only way, night will turn to day, no matter what they say, sing and smile and pray, that's the only way, if we sing and smile and pray, we'll drive the clouds away."

We continued to sing and smile and pray. The wind blew the little clouds of raindrops passed us and we were kept dry by God's grace. The children were amazed that God cared enough to answer our little prayer song and meet our special needs.

**What a blessing it was to use this teachable moment
to impress my children
with the fact that we have a great God
who loves and cares for us all the time,
in every circumstance.**

Together in a Miracle

Michele seemed troubled one night as I sat on her bed, getting ready for our prayer time. When I asked what was wrong she told me that her best friend told her, while they were playing together that day, that her daddy and mommy were getting a divorce. I asked her what that meant to see what she understood. She was only three years old at the time but intelligent beyond her years. Michele said that her friend said it meant her daddy could not live with her and her mother anymore. The thought had been on Michele's mind most of day and she feared that one day her daddy might go away.

I led in prayer and then she prayed. I will never forget what she asked of the Lord, "Please keep my Daddy and Mama together in a miracle." Through the years of marriage problems, I have remembered those words and prayed them myself. I told her one day when she was older that she and the Lord were responsible for keeping David and me together in a miracle. It is true. No matter what the devil did to destroy our marriage, our sanity, our emotions, our finances, our children, our home or our ministry, God has not allowed the evil one to go any further than the short leash that controls him.

The battle has been the Lord's and He fought to keep us together in His great power.

-47-

MICHELE'S SALVATION

We lived in Buford, GA three years. From the time Michele was about four years old, she had asked many questions about becoming a Christian. At age six, she asked me one afternoon if God talked to us. I knew God had a special answer for her, so I asked her did she think He could. She said, "Yes," and then she quickly gave the answer the Lord gave her. I wished I had that statement on tape. It was a beautiful answer. David and I had talked to her several times about the Lord and His place in our lives.

One night at bedtime, she was troubled as she had been many times before. One reason was because she did not want to go to bed. The second reason was she was afraid of the dark and thought she saw a tall man in her room. We talked a while until she felt more secure. Then she said she wished she could become a Christian, but could not because she did not know everything about the Bible yet like "Mama and Daddy did." I had not realized that had been worrying her. I explained that we did not know everything about the Bible either, but we knew the Lord Jesus. I explained how she could ask the Lord to save her right there in her bedroom. We talked about her sin and the remedy being the blood the Lord shed to cover our sin. She prayed and asked the Lord to save her. It was a wonderful miracle! I took her upstairs and ask her to tell her daddy what had just happened. It was her first opportunity to be a witness of what the Lord had done in her life.

She and I were making cookies one morning when she asked me to tell her about the day Jesus died. As I got to the part of the story about the day becoming dark as night, the Lord sent a dark cloud to hide the sunshine. Michele asked if that day was dark like the one we were having. I said it was, but much darker.

**How wonderful of the Lord to set the stage
with perfect lighting to make the story more vivid for us!**

Ask Yourself...

What teachable moments has God given me to impress my children and others with His great love and care for us no matter what the circumstances?

Record these events in your journal and watch for more opportunities God gives you throughout each day.

Read Proverbs 22:6.

What is God's promise to you for your children if you obey His instructions?

PART EIGHT
MINISTRY MIRACLES

-48-

EXTENDED LIFE

While David was Minister of Music at First Baptist Church, McCaysville, GA, we had many lovely experiences working with the folks in that congregation. Some of them were from McCaysville and others were from the adjoining town of Copperhill, TN. The State line ran through the middle of the town, right through the parking lot of two grocery stores. On the McCaysville, GA side, the store charged state sales tax. On the other side of the parking lot, just over the State line, there was no sales tax in Tennessee.

One day in the ladies Sunday School class, several of the women requested prayer for members of the church. We bowed to have special prayer for Jean, a sweet lady who had brain cancer. The teacher brought us up to date on her condition, telling us the doctor had said it was "just a matter of time" before she passed away. As we took turns praying, every lady in the class prayed for the family to be comforted and to be prepared for her death in the next few days. When it was my time to pray, I felt the Lord telling me to pray for her to live. I asked the Lord to allow her to live another year until her daughter graduated from High School. The daughter needed her mother's strong Christian guidance. I wanted her mother to be in her life and have a chance to help her make wise choices. I did not feel the daughter was ready for her mother to be taken at that point in her life.

God was gracious to answer the prayer He had prompted with a "yes." Jean lived two more years! By that time her daughter was out of High School and a bit more stable in her teenage life. Jean suffered with another brain tumor, but I thank God for her life and influence in her family and in our church as we witnessed her sweet spirit through her illness.

-49-

THE TRIP TO ISRAEL AND ROME

In 1973 the Georgia Sons of Jubal, men's singing group, made up of Ministers of Music, were invited by Israel's Minister of Tourism to come to Israel and sing worship concerts in churches and kibbutz. A two-day sight-seeing trip to Rome was also to be a part of the trip. The wives of the men were encouraged to go as a part of the tour. Many of us were in the Georgia Baptist State women's group, the Jubalheirs, and were asked to learn some songs in Hebrew to sing with the Sons of Jubal when they visited in the kibbutz. Even Michele, five years old at the time, and Michael, three years old, learned the songs and remembered them as they grew up.

The expenses for the men in the choral group were being paid by the churches they served as Ministers of Music. David was Minister of Music at First Baptist Church, Buford, GA at that time. The congregation voted to pay David's expenses so he could be a part of the mission trip. Each family member who went on the trip was to pay his or her expenses. We knew we did not have the finances for me to make the trip. We prayed I would get to go if it was God's will and that He would provide the funds. I prayed that it would work out if I could benefit from the trip or use what I learned to help others in their spiritual growth. I was eager to learn more about the land where Jesus lived and believed the experience would help me be a more effective Bible teacher and student of the Word.

Two weeks before the $600.00 was due for the trip, I had a pastor at the GA Baptist State Convention give me a dime toward the trip as he laughed about the fact there was no way I would get to go. That year for Christmas, my uncles and aunts from Savannah and relatives in Pembroke who normally gave our family presents bought gifts for our children and gave money toward my trip overseas. A friend of ours who worked with my mother at the local bank gave one-third of the total trip cost. We sent the money to the GA Baptist Convention Church Music Department office, a few days before the deadline for the trip.

**Again, the Lord provided for us and answered
our prayers just in time.**

THE PIANO

While living in Buford, GA, a friend of ours noticed that David would pack us all in the car to drive to the church each time we needed to practice our duets because we did not have a piano. The friend was a pastor and a jack-of-all-trades. He played piano in a restaurant each week near Buford. One night, he called David to tell him he had an old upright piano in a theater that he owned. The man wanted to give it to us, so we could practice at home and the family would not be inconvenienced. What a thoughtful thing to do as prompted by the Lord to help our family.

Years later, David borrowed $500.00 from a Christian lawyer who was a member of the church in Pompano where David served as Minister of Music. He had paid back $300 in three months, then he was asked to leave the church by a group of four men who had "come to power" after our pastor had been called to serve a church in Crestview, FL. We attended a Good Friday service at Coral Ridge Presbyterian Church the week David "resigned." When the offering plate was passed, I gave my last $2.00. David did not have any money with him.

I asked the Lord to bless the gift one hundredfold. Then I quickly said, "Lord, I do not mean for you to give us $200.00, but use the money to further your Kingdom." He spoke to my spirit and let me know He could help others and help us as well. I was so excited! When David asked if that was the last money I had, I told him that it was, but God was going to give us back $200.00! He wondered why I was so sure, but the Lord had let me know and I knew it would come to pass.

About two weeks later, the lawyer called David to tell him he did not want him to repay him the last $200.00. Instead, he wanted David to find someone who had a child that could not afford piano lessons and give them $200.00 worth of piano lessons. David knew a lady in our church who had low income and two daughters who he could teach piano. He taught them on the piano our Buford friend had given us a few years before.

God called us to a church in Jacksonville a short time later. The upright piano was so heavy that David did not want us to move it one more time. He said he felt the Lord wanted him to give the piano to the lady and her daughters.

What a blessing the piano had been to us through the years and continued to be for the Dorey family.

RECESSION

During the recession in 1974, our finances were tight and we were having a hard time getting by on David's salary. I considered meat too expensive so usually left it off my grocery list. I had promised the Lord when we had children, I would stay home with them unless He sent me a job outside the home. One day, I received a call from the secretary of the Superintendent of Schools telling me they had two job openings at the elementary school and they wanted to hire the Superintendent's wife and me. I was to take a cart with a record player and songbooks from room to room, teaching the children the songs suggested for their grade level.

**God provided additional income for us so I could
buy groceries
and help pay a bank loan we had for our home.**

The tithes and offerings always came out first before I bought anything we needed. After all, everything we have has been given to us from the Father.

CALL TO SOUTH FLORIDA

David was called by a Baptist church in Pompano Beach, FL in August to be their Minister of Music. Michael's allergies became worse living there, probably due to the tropical flowers and trees in that area. He was getting sick about every six weeks and given a prescription for medicine that had to constantly be refilled.

When he swallowed the last dose of the medicine, I told him I was going to pray that Jesus would heal him unless there was a reason He would be glorified in the illness. In faith, I told him we would not have to refill the medicine again. Trusting God, I put Michael's empty medicine bottle on the shelf above our kitchen sink to remind us of his healing we had claimed.

The doctor had told us it would take Michael about a year to adjust to the pollens in the area, but we never had to refill the prescription again!

-53-

New Direction for Ministry

While I was serving as Dean of Women at the Youth Music Camp at Lake Yale Baptist Assembly in the summer of 1982, Earl Berry, Director of Camps and Assemblies Department for the Florida Baptist Convention, asked me to meet with him in his office. He had been a friend of ours since we were students at Southwestern Baptist Theological Seminary in Ft. Worth, TX. After working on the staff at several churches, he was led to work with camps and assemblies in Florida. We had known his wife from contact with her at the snack area on the seminary campus where she cooked our "lunches grabbed on the run" between classes. Each time we attended conferences at Lake Yale with our church groups, we would spend some time visiting with E. B. and his wife over a cup of tea or at mealtime.

The morning I came over to talk with Earl, he explained he had contacted a camp manager in TX to take the leadership position as manager of the new camp in Marianna, FL. The well-qualified manager had said he was willing to take the position, although his wife was not in favor of the move. Sometime later, Earl realized it was not God's will for this man to take that job. He prayed the Texan would call him back and tell him he felt he should not come. His prayer was answered. The manager called and said he would not be able to move to Florida since his wife was not in agreement with him and did not think it was best for them.

He told me he then remembered talking with David a few years before about working in camps and assemblies. Earl felt strongly that he should speak to David about taking the job and asked me to have David contact him after we had time to pray together about the offer. When I returned home from camp at the end of the week, I told David what Earl had discussed with me. He said he had been thinking for the past two weeks that he could not continue doing the youth and music combination work he had been doing at his home church for about three years. It had been a strain on our family life as he poured all his energies into his work, being all things to all people, and having nothing left for the children and me. The camp work had been on his mind and he had wondered if he should contact Earl and talk with him about a position at Lake Yale.

The next week, he contacted Earl and we met with him in our home to discuss the job requirements. The job would necessitate our moving to Blue Springs Baptist Assembly in Marianna, FL, and living in the spacious apartment above the office. As resident Manager, David would be on the job or on call 24 hours a day with little free time. I would be busy as secretary. Earl's boss from the Florida Baptist Convention met with us for lunch the next week. It was a comedy of errors as our meals got mixed up by the waitress and instead of sending them back, we ate meals we did not order.

There was a lot of laughter and when we shook hands and said goodbye, I told David, "I think that was our job interview."

As we walked to our vehicles, Earl's boss told him that we had been hired. He had been interested in seeing if we had a good sense of humor. He said if we did not have a sense of humor we would not be successful serving Florida Baptists and other groups of conferees with the challenges that came with the job.

-54-

A Dark Quiet Place in the Woods

During the trials in the church on the South side of Jacksonville, I had been praying, "Lord, I need a dark, quiet place in the woods, about a mile off the road where David and I can be with our family and re-group. I'd like to stay home, but would also like to help David with the income if needed and if that is Your will."

The city traffic in Jacksonville was so noisy at night when we were trying to rest, I had longed for a special "quiet place." So many concerns were in my mind and heart. The Lord had already begun to answer these prayers and much more.

One thing I thought we needed was better insurance in case David died and I had to make a living for the family. We had never been to Blue Springs Baptist Assembly in Marianna, Florida, until June of 1982. We were on the way to the Southern Baptist Convention annual meeting held in New Orleans, LA, to sing as a part of the Florida Baptist Singing Men and Women. We spent one night with the group of singers at the assembly and had two meals in the dining hall before continuing on the chartered bus to the SBC convention meeting. How amazing, just three months later, that God put us in charge of the facility!

We moved to the assembly grounds in September of 1982. Our children finished the first week of school in Jacksonville and then took a bus to Marianna. It was the first time we had moved that they had not been responsible for helping pack and unpack our belongings. We picked them up at the bus station and took them to the assembly to show them around. They were so impressed to see that we had their bedrooms all set up and they had new bedspreads and accessories. Our daughter was so glad that the hard work was done and everything was in place. The children did not realize how much work was ahead of us as we started our new assignment. None of us could have imaged that.

After moving to Marianna, I realized that while I was praying for "a dark, quiet place in the woods," over the two-year period, ground was being broken and buildings were being constructed at Blue Springs Baptist Assembly in Marianna, FL. It took just about two years to complete the facilities. God began answering as I prayed.

God began to "prepare" a place for us where we could be "stewards of many things, due to being faithful over a few things" in the past.

It was a place built by others for us to share with people throughout the State of Florida and the nation, increasing our borders, and enlarging our ministry for Him.

-55-

YEARS OF PREPARATION

We had been prepared throughout our lives for this type ministry. Growing up in our community, I had been asked to sing in all the churches ministering with people in all the churches in our community, ministering with people from different denominations. Each year, my brother and I went to three weeks of Vacation Bible School held in the various churches in Pembroke, as well as our own Baptist church.

Buddy and I went to Christian Camp at Shellman Bluff near Glennville, Georgia, for eight years which was a summer camp sponsored by the Christian Church Association. We had attended summer camps at Ridgecrest Baptist Assembly, in North Carolina, with our church sponsors.

As I grew up in Pembroke, my mother and I were asked to sing at funerals in churches of different denominations in our community. Many times, she had to get me out of school to be a part of this special ministry to those who needed comfort and hope and had asked us to sing.

David and I both had scholarships working in the kitchen at the small Georgia colleges we attended. He went to Norman Park Junior College in Moultrie, Georgia, and I went to Tift College in Forsyth, Georgia. Little did we know that one day we would be in charge of food service for hundreds of people, overseeing a commercial size kitchen with sophisticated equipment and a dining room with seating for 300. When the Youth Camp was built, we had the capacity of serving 200 persons in that area.

These experiences were used by God and multiplied our service.

We went through periods of being broken and spilled out for Him as we became more fully the servants of the Most High God. We became the gatekeepers as mentioned in 1 Chronicles 9:23-29. We were the overseers of the buildings, the rooms, the lodging, the vessels, the instruments of the sanctuary, the fine flour, oil, spices, and thereby, ministered to the strangers within our gates.

God used the musical abilities that He gave us, allowing us to sing together, play handbells, and provide service music in various churches and at the State Assembly when the groups needed musical leadership. We also worked in the summer youth music camps teaching classes and were available as youth counselors in the dorms as we had done at the Georgia Baptist Assembly in Toccoa, Georgia, and Lake Yale Baptist Assembly in Eustis, FL. On the grounds of the assembly, we had a ministry outside the local church where David and I could use our musical talents and he could play the piano or organ for groups as needed.

He also used his Sign Language skills working with the Deaf through First Baptist Church, Marianna, where our family became members and in the public school system. He and I sang in the choir together and took part in the ministries of the church. We had not been able to sing in choirs together for years, due his responsibilities in music leadership as Minister of Music for sixteen years in churches in Georgia and Florida.

At BSBA, I was in a place where I could be at home and also help with the income, something I had always wanted to do. The salary package included insurance coverage for our family which had been one of my concerns. We would live upstairs over the office area in a totally electric, three bedroom and two bath apartment, larger than the house we had in Jacksonville. "Home" was sixteen steps away from work. Some days that was an advantage and other days we were too accessible to the public through the office, though most of them did not know how to get to our apartment. There were 125 acres to oversee, later increasing to 150 acres, where there was "room enough to receive" all God's blessings He had for us as He continued to answer my prayers.

There were one hundred rooms in the adult motel located in three buildings. I was reminded of the scripture, "in my Father's house are many mansions." The Lord spoke to me through several scriptures as I saw what He had planned for us to do. David had been pressured for a year by a pastor friend in Jacksonville to buy a home and felt like a failure because he could not do so. I told him, "Do not worry about a house. If God wants us to have one, He will give it to us." The Lord spoke again to us through those simple words and brought it to pass as we moved into the apartment above the office at Blue Springs Baptist Assembly. We did not have to rent or buy a home, just work hard and we were allowed to live in the place He provided for us. Confirmation of our call would come for months after we moved in and started the work there.

"Strangers within our gates" would say as they checked in at the desk for conferences, "God has sent you to this place. It is so evident."

I would reply, "I know," and give my testimony about praying for the dark, quiet place in the woods where we could serve the Lord as a family. It was so quiet at night, I could not hear the wind blow or even hear birds singing. I remember talking to the Lord one day and saying, "Lord, I would like to hear the birds sing." Soon, the Lord sent the birds to sing for me and build a nest on our deck upstairs in the safe places they found in the nooks and crannies.

The previous manager, Mr. Ridgeway, and his wife, stayed on the job for two weeks to train us in the basics of the job. When they moved away, their daughter who had been helping cook in the Adult Assembly and her friend, moved also. That left us with no cooks to prepare food for the groups coming in for our first weekend of leadership. On staff, we had a part-time maintenance man who was not well-trained. There were two housekeepers to clean the one hundred motel rooms, wash, dry, and fold the linens for the conferees to use, clean the cafeteria, the kitchen, twelve conference rooms, office areas, and auditorium.

David, our children, Michele (a ninth-grader), Michael (a seventh-grader), and I cooked three meals for the 200 conferees Friday night through Saturday lunch. I registered the conferees, gave them their room keys, dealt with their questions, and answered the phones while David helped our children prepare meals. When I finished the office work, I joined them cooking and serving meals. After each meal, we all helped clean up the dining room, kitchen, dish room, and put all the clean dishes back in place for the next meal. We worked eleven and a half hours on that first Saturday with a thirty-minute break.

Michele said God might have called David and me to do that work, but He did not call her! She and Michael had a lot of adjustments to make. They said one problem was that we did not have neighbors. The grounds covered 125 acres and none of their friends lived nearby. Transportation for Michele and Michael to the Friday night football games was a problem also since David and I both worked during the week and especially on weekends. Both children were in the band and were required to be at the games on Friday nights. In his last two years of high school, Michael played football and Michele played in the band, so we had to get rides for them.

David's folks bought a new car and gave their grandchildren the "old" car to share to help with transportation after Michele got her driver's license. That was a gracious act and an answer to prayer. In 1986, the camp facilities in Panama City, FL, were sold and the youth camp was built at our assembly, another answer to my prayers. I had worked in the Young Musician camp each summer in Panama City teaching ukulele and a music class. The facilities there were run down and I prayed it could be sold so the camps could be held at BSBA. With the building of the Youth Camp, our responsibilities increased. We were then overseers of two camps and two kitchens, needing additional staff operating on a small budget under the Florida Baptist Convention guidelines.

We continued to be stewards "over many things" in His name as He gave us strength. Michael was fourteen years old when the Youth Camp was being built at the assembly on the lake side of the property. He was hired to lay pipe along with other jobs and learned quite a bit about manual labor as he worked in the hot sun. He learned quickly why I told him his first paycheck should be spent on steel-toed shoes. He saw no need in getting the shoes, but one accident taught him that lesson and made a lasting impression. He and the maintenance man's son cleaned out the lake area to get it ready for swimming for the youth and adults who would soon be housed in the camp. Alligators were usually present as they worked on the water's edge and followed the boys back and forth as they cleared the area along the bank.

The boys watched carefully as the angels kept watch over the boys.

Training at Lake Yale

In September of 1988, Mr. B., David's supervisor and Director of Properties and Camps and Assemblies, worked out a plan for David to get some required maintenance training. This necessitated our move to Lake Yale Baptist Assembly (later named Lake Yale Conference Center) near Eustis and Leesburg, FL, where Mr. B. was Manager of LYBA. This was a great adjustment in my life. Michele graduated from Junior College and moved to Jacksonville, FL, May 6, 1988. My step-father died May 31. Michael graduated from Jackson County High School June 1 and enlisted in the Army, taking a delayed entry dated September 13. We took Michael to the bus station to catch a bus to Montgomery, AL, where he was to be processed into the Army. He was to then catch a flight to Atlanta and go on to Ft. Sill, OK, for Boot Camp and A.I.T. (Advanced Individual Training).

The day we took him to the bus station, we left for Lake Yale to choose housing available there on the grounds. Our move was scheduled for October 12, Columbus Day. We were in search of a "new" home much like Columbus had been looking for a new world. The last week of September, my aunt from Savannah, GA, died after a long incurable illness. David and I made arrangements to attend the service and sing at the funeral. Those five months caused a strain on our emotions as we made the necessary adjustments.

The Lake Yale Baptist Assembly staff accepted us as fellow workers and in a short period of time we felt a part of the team. We appreciated getting to know the staff on a personal basis. David worked in Food Service with Emory Gnann, and later with

Sherry Maier. He also worked in Maintenance with Jim Smith and Ed Graham. Then he worked in Office Management with Charlie Goen and Earl Berry. Office assistants Kay, Charlene, and Margie were helpful as David learned office management and had computer training.

Virginia Edwards had asked me to help her at the Lifeway Book Store, formerly the Baptist Book Store. She knew I had experience working at the Baptist Book Store on the seminary campus in Ft. Worth, TX. She needed me to relieve her especially when the store was open at night. The work was enjoyable and it was great to get to visit with many of the conferees, various language groups, and friends who came to the scheduled retreats.

"The Lord does work in mysterious ways, His wonders to perform" and in the "fullness of time" there arose a great need at Blue Springs Baptist Assembly.

In a few months, Mr. Berry made David aware of the need and the possibility that we would be moving back to manage the Assembly in Marianna. David was called to the office one day to talk with Mr. Berry. Knowing the situation at Blue Springs Baptist Assembly and the need for leadership at Lake Yale when Earl retired, David stopped by our trailer to ask me to pray we could stay at Lake Yale.

I knelt to pray and said, "Lord, David wants me to pray that we will be able to stay at Lake Yale." At that point, I stopped praying because the Lord showed me a vision in my spirit. It was an 8 X 10 picture of the two of us that we had on our living room bookcase. In the vision, the picture was located at the registration desk at Blue Springs Baptist Assembly and a caption underneath the picture read "UNDER FORMER MANAGEMENT."

At that point, I got up from my knees and began packing my favorite pictures and books from the bookcase in the living room. When David came home from his meeting with Mr. Berry, he asked me if I had prayed. I told him what had happened and that I knew we were going to move. That was why I was packing.

**He said there was no way I could not know that,
but I told him about the vision I had and
I knew it was going to happen as the Lord had shown me.**

The next day, the boss made the decision that one of the former maintenance men who had been sent to Blue Springs Baptist Assembly as Manager was to be moved back to Lake Yale. We were needed to move back to our former residence and live in the apartment over the office at Blue Springs Baptist Assembly.

RETURN TO BLUE SPRINGS

On August 29, 1989, ten months after we moved to Lake Yale Baptist Assembly, the Lake Yale staff helped us put our personal belongings on a big U Haul truck and we began our five and a half-hour trip back to BSBA. Coming back after the training period, David felt more confident in being the leader of the assembly. In some ways, it was like coming home although our children had moved away and things had changed at the assembly.

Our church friends from First Baptist Church, Marianna, seemed very pleased to have us "back where we belonged" according to their quote. It was a lovely experience to be so warmly welcomed. The Singles Department from First Baptist Church, Marianna, had been praying for our return for the 10 months we had been gone, according to one of the members of that department who was also in David's Handbell Choir.

How lovely to see God's hand of direction.

We moved back to serve Him at Blue Springs and at First Baptist Church. Our first Wednesday back, we attended the handbell rehearsal and David was asked again to take the leadership of the group. It was as if we had never been gone. We joined the church the following Sunday and joined the Choir taking our former places in the alto and tenor sections. So, for the second time, we were entrusted with 125 acres of pine and oak trees, beautiful, especially when the rain swept through the property and we could stand in the apartment upstairs looking out on the grounds. The view from that level was even lovelier than I had remembered.

Business picked up at the assembly and in a few weeks, we were anticipating our busiest September and October ever. A few new workers were hired to get us through quick changes as 200 people checked in, stayed two days, and checked out with 200 more checking in the same day. All the 100 motel rooms, 12 conference rooms, 400-seat auditorium, dining hall, and grounds had to be cleaned and ready for the next group. All the sheets, towels, etc. had to be washed in our commercial laundry on site. I usually did the laundry by myself, though occasionally someone came to help fold the sheets. The laundry was an important part of getting the motel ready for use and usually was a two-day job just doing sheets.

We served about 800 people that week in September with our small staff, serving 3200 meals. It is no wonder my theme song during that time was "The Joy of the Lord is My Strength" and the second like unto it, a line from the Kenny Rogers hit, "You've gotta know when to fold 'em, know when to hold 'em." My favorite part of the song came at the end of the day, when I sang, "Know when to walk away."

For twelve years, the busiest time of the year was the last week in April, Thursday through Saturday, when 500 women from First Pentecostal Church, Pensacola, FL, came to the campus for a prayer retreat. What a wonderful spirited group and the most cooperative you could ask for! We housed as many as we could in the Adult motel and Youth Camp, while others made reservations in Marianna motels. They came together at the assembly for meetings and meals. I called it the "feeding of the 5,000." Some of our workers believed we had really fed 5,000 people! Actually, we fed 500 people six meals for a total of 3,000 meals, about double the number our facility could accommodate!

About six weeks after our return to Marianna, the Minister of Music at our church resigned. The church needed someone to serve in music leadership and asked David to become the Interim Minister of Music. He was allowed to lead in this capacity for only two months due to FL Baptist Convention policies and procedures governing service other than Convention job assignments. He was asked to lead the handbell choir the week we had returned and was already working in that area. One of the ringers jokingly told him, "You sure have missed a lot of rehearsals." Years before our daughter, David and I rang in that group. Now David was ringing as needed and directing the group and I was ringing bells again. One of the handbell ringers said for ten months she had prayed we would move back to Marianna and David would direct the bell choir again.

God had worked all the experiences for His glory and our good to bring us back to a place of former service.

Signing Wonders

My morning felt unusually blessed with God's presence. I had prayed the Lord would use me in a mighty way as I sang "Hallelujah, Praise the Lamb" solo in the morning church service. I was also singing on Praise Team that day. I told the Minister of Music that the Lord had a great chance to be made strong in weakness when He used me to sing or do whatever He asked. I was reminded of the scripture in 2 Corinthians 12:9 where He tells us His strength is made perfect in weakness.

How wonderful to know when I am weak He is strong.

I practiced the music for the service with the Praise Team and then went to my Sunday School class. After being in the class for only about five minutes, Mark, my Minister of Music, came by the class and asked if he could see me for a minute. Bill O'Brien, a Christian deaf man I met in Wal-Mart seven months before, was at church. I had helped him communicate with the Pharmacist concerning his medication and insurance coverage. He was from Greenwood and needed a job, so he applied for a job while he was there. I was available to help him with that situation also.

God had me in the right place at the right time.

I had invited him to our church and told him my husband was an interpreter for the deaf. Many times, David was not at church due to staying home to care for his mother at that time in our lives. This particular day, Bill decided to come to our church and anticipated David being there to interpret. We did not know he was coming and no one at the church knew any sign language but me. When I saw Bill at the front door, I recognized him and told the Minister of Music that I knew him. I introduced him to the Minister of Music, the Pastor, and our church secretary. He signed to them, but they could not understand so I tried my best to interpret for all of them. It was easy to read his signs and he had some ability to speak, so communication was not as difficult as it could have been for us.

During the Sunday School hour, Bill decided to go get some breakfast and returned later for the church service. He was surprised that my husband was not there. I explained that he was at home taking care of his mother and although I was not an interpreter, I was willing to do what I could to help him understand the service. I told him that I would be on the platform, singing with the Praise Team, for the first part of the service.

He sat in the congregation and watched carefully as we began the song service. I signed as a friend held my microphone and he copied my signs as he took part in the "music." The pastor led us in prayer and I interpreted the prayer for Bill. That Sunday, I had been asked to sing a solo and felt for a week or so I should sign the chorus, not knowing the Lord was leading my thinking and was going to pour out a special blessing on me. I came to the mike and signed to him that I was singing, "Hallelujah, Praise the Lamb." He knew the song and watched me closely as I sang. When I came to the chorus I turned toward him and signed. He copied me and signed also. It was so exciting to me. As I finished the last part of the song, I looked out toward others in the congregation and did not see Bill as he stood in reverence to the Lamb of God of whom I sang. I did not know until later that Bill had stood and touched the hearts of several people who saw him standing in worship.

A doctor, who had been in the congregation, told me at my appointment with him the next week, about Bill's response in the service and how it touched him spiritually.

When the Praise Team members sat down in the congregation, I sat beside Bill instead of standing in front as many interpreters do. I did not want the attention on me. I was only there to be used of the Lord and interpret for Bill. It was the first time I had ever needed to interpret a sermon. Bill was kind and encouraging as I attempted to put the words of the pastor into sign language so he could understand the message. If I needed him to help me with a sign, I spelled the word I questioned and he gave me the sign. He was very helpful and put me at ease. I kept remembering I had prayed early that morning for the Lord to use me in a mighty way. It was thrilling to be used of the Lord in that amazing situation! He had to do what was done that day because I was not qualified to be an interpreter. However, I was available and God used me. I could not see how that day could be any better!

On the way home from church, I was listening to my favorite Christian radio station and I heard the choral arrangement of my favorite song, "His Eye is On the Sparrow!" I could hardly believe it! He definitely was watching over me, as He always does, but in an awesome way that day, giving me life abundantly. I have learned more and more about the abundant life through trials and problems I have faced. He is my life, my all. He gives abundant life of joy that far outweighs the things of earth that challenge us and even the good things.

He is all I need as I willingly give up my life for Him to use and work through to bring Him glory. Praise His Name!

125

Ask Yourself...

Am I willingly give up my life for Him to use and work through to bring Him glory?

Record in your journal what giving up your life to Him means and how you see Him moving toward bringing Him glory.

Read 2 Corinthians 12:9.

What is God's promise to you in this verse?

PART NINE
GOD'S AMAZING
PROVISION MIRACLES

Pick Up Your Bed and Walk

While in Pompano Beach, Florida, serving North Pompano Baptist Church, we felt it best to rent and live within the housing allowance we were provided. The week we moved to Pompano Beach, a small temporary house with only four rooms was made available at no cost to us by a member of the church where David worked. Most of our furniture was put in storage. Michele started first grade and Michael went to our church kindergarten.

We soon found a nice three-bedroom, two-bath house in a good neighborhood. Bill Sears, the owner, did not want to rent the house due to problems he had with past renters. However, he did decide to accept us as renters. Bill came over each week to work on the house. About a month after we moved in, he told me he had decided to sell the house. I had just finished hemming the curtains in our living room and had the house in good order. This situation meant we would have to move and Michele probably had to change schools in the fall. Michael would be going into First Grade. Although we were disappointed in having to be uprooted again, we knew the Lord would provide schools for the children and a place for us to live.

A new adventure in faith began.

-60-

THE MATTHEWS HOUSE

Ms. Matthews, a member of the church where David served as Minister of Music, told fellow church members, Hollis and Clarinda Rule, her husband had moved to Virginia to find work as a carpenter. She was moving to be with him because she had heart problems and did not need to stay alone. She was looking for a family that would rent and take care of the house.

Friends told her we needed a place to rent and set up a meeting with her to discuss the matter. She agreed to let us rent the house for the monthly amount the church provided for our housing allowance. Michele and Michael entered a new school having only a few blocks to walk each day.

The house had four bedrooms and two baths. The yard was covered with lovely flowers and trees. We felt right at home and were glad to be settled at last. After living in the house only ten months, Mr. Matthews' job was finished and he could not find more work to sustain his income. Ms. Matthews called us and said they would need to move back to their house in a few weeks. I told the children we had to move again. Michele asked me one night before we had our goodnight prayers if she would have to change schools. Normally, I would have told her we would pray about it and Jesus would let us know, but that night I heard myself saying, "No, you will not have to change schools." Then I wondered why I had sounded so certain. I accepted that as God's answer to me.

**God allowed me to speak with assurance because
she would not have to change schools.**

-61-

HOUSE WITH A POOL

We began to pray about finding a house near the same school the children attended. A small house near the school became available. We took a tour of the house with the Christian realtor and told her we would like to rent it. The day we were to sign the lease with her, another realtor who knew we needed a house, called to say a house had just been put on the market that she wanted us to see. The Christian realtor had the papers ready to sign but insisted we look at the other house, in case that was God's house for us. Since it was a nicer home and nearer our children's school, we decided to go see it. It was total electric and the cleanest house we had seen so far. It seemed we should tell the realtor that we would take that house.

In the meantime, the pastor of our church felt God calling him to a new church field on Florida's West Coast and asked if we would consider living in that home, pending approval of the church leaders. Within a week, the leaders told us the house was being kept for the next pastor. We called the realtor to tell her we would take the house she had shown us. By that time, it was no longer available and the small one had been leased as well.

Through prayer, we felt led to call a realtor about a house for sale that was nearer the children's school. We could not buy it but asked him to see if the owner, Ms. Swenson, would rent the house to us. He said his client was hard to deal with, but he would ask. Her husband was a drug dealer and she had a bad reputation in the community. Several times a week, the neighbors would call the police to come break up the rowdy parties at the house. Ms.

Swenson told the realtor she wanted $600.00 a month rent. He was certain she would not consider less.

I felt strongly God was leading us to rent that house. I told the realtor we would like to offer the owner $300.00 a month, the amount of our housing allowance the church provided. The realtor was surprised that I would think the owner would accept such a proposal. I told him I had prayed in faith the amount would be accepted. He had his doubts but told me to go ahead and call the owner.

When I presented my offer to her over the phone and told her I had prayed about what God would have us do, she said she would rent the house to us for $300.00 a month, half of what she had wanted! God turned her heart toward us and sent us a miracle! The realtor was amazed! He realized God had answered prayer but found it hard to believe that she had said "Yes!"

I reminded him I had prayed and God had worked it out for us.

On the same day, we had to move out of Ms. Matthews' house, we were allowed to move into the two-story house with a screened-in swimming pool, in the same block as the school! God's provision and timing were perfect! The neighbors were so glad to have us. The mailman would come up to the mailbox cautiously each day, wondering if what he had heard was true, that the former owner had moved out. I invited him in one day to see the changes we had made in the house.

His reply was interesting, "I would not go in that house. Have you prayed the demons out of it?"

From the stories people told us about the activities that went on in the house prior to our moving in, we could understand his concern. It was interesting as we walked passed the cork wall in the hallway to find it had absorbed the drug odors, a scent we had never experienced before. Our youth from the church teased us about "sniffing our walls" when they came over for a swimming party at our house from time to time.

-62-

JOB PROVISION

A few months later, due to a lack of finances in our church and divisive spirits in the leadership, my husband was asked to resign his staff position. He was called back to the church by leaders of the church around 10:00 o'clock after he had led the Prayer Meeting service on a Wednesday night. When he arrived at the church, he saw several members driving their cars out of the parking lot as quickly as possible, so as not to face him. There were only four men left to talk with him when he went to his office. He asked why he was being dismissed and the only answer he received was, "It's not working out." We realized later the plan the men had was to pay one person to fill three positions of the staff. Therefore, they planned to ask David to leave, and hire an independently wealthy pastor. These were the same men who had told him what a good job he was doing after the church service that same night. One of them had taken David and Michael to the Miami Dolphins football game just a few weeks before.

Our pastor had been called to another church a short time prior to David being asked to leave. Men who had been inactive members of the church were asked to assume leadership positions after the pastor moved out of town. The lack of tithes and offerings from the members resulted in the staff having problems paying the bills of the church and meeting the expenses of the Christian school that was a part of the complex. Staff members received their salaries on a rotating basis depending on the offerings received each week. The only staff member who was always paid each week was the janitor.

The deacons had asked David to preach as well as continue his duties as Minister of Music and Youth making him the only full-time paid staff member. He had told the deacons that he was not called to preach, but he did perform a wedding after the pastor moved to West Florida. He brought the message for a young boy's funeral who was a member of the church and led in the Lord's Supper services.

At the time, I was working in a non-denominational Christian school from which I received a small income. School was to be out for the summer in a few weeks and it looked as though we would not have my income at that point. David was very upset about his situation and wondered how we would pay our bills that month. As I prayed about the situation, I felt covered in a protective bubble and knew everything was going to work out in God's time. I assured David that within two weeks, the time he was due for paid vacation in his benefit package, he would have a job.

The Lord gave me that knowledge in my spirit.

Friends from the church gave us a luncheon and presented us with a money tree. Those funds helped us pay the bills for the month. With David's severance package, the two weeks paid vacation, my school salary, and the salary from David's new job two weeks later, we had more money that month than we ever had before!

The Lord worked in mysterious ways performing miracles for His glory!

Two weeks later, David was hired as Interim Minister of Music, Youth Leader, and Janitor in Plantation, FL. The job was considered part-time, yet David was paid a full-time salary with benefits! We still had our house in Pompano Beach and did not have to move.

We commuted to the church in Plantation twice a week for services. The church owned a house next door to the church. On the lot was a swimming pool. Our family was allowed to stay in the house on the weekends as needed, enjoy the pool, and save on expenses.

We loved the people of that fellowship and found Christian love in abundance. The pastor of the church was a great fellow with whom to work and well-known in that area. He had even witnessed to members of criminal gangs in South Florida and was available to everyone.

A HOME PROVIDED

About two months later, David was called to his hometown to be the Minister of Music and Youth near the St. Johns Park area in Jacksonville, FL. A home became available for us due to unusual circumstances. The bookkeeper at the church owned a house he had planned to sell but decided to rent it to us. It joined the lot where he lived and was in need of repairs, which he worked on from time to time. He became our landlord and took out the small amount of rent money from David's salary check before David was paid each month.

God continued providing for all our needs in amazing ways!

The house was across the street from Publix grocery store at the Roosevelt Shopping Mall and near the church. I could buy groceries, push the grocery cart home, unload it, and return the cart to the store. Our church where David worked and the school where our children were enrolled were only a few blocks away, within walking distance! This was very convenient since we only had one vehicle.

-64-

MIRACLE JOB

David had been having trouble through the years with his back due to an injury that occurred while he was helping move a large rug up a flight of stairs at the church in Pompano where he was Minister of Music. His back problems worsened to the point he needed medical treatment. The day we understood it would be necessary for months of treatments, we prayed for the funds to be made available to help us pay for the charges involved.

Before going to bed that Wednesday night, I prayed the Lord would let me know if He wanted me work part-time to pay the medical expenses. I asked that the Lord send the job to me, as all my jobs outside the home had been sent to me after we had children. My priority was being a full-time wife and mother. I asked specifically that the job be near our home, that it would not interfere with our church life, the use of the one car we shared, or take me away from my responsibilities and privileges in my home.

The next afternoon, I was called by Florida Junior College, Kent Campus, Jacksonville, FL, to teach a class in World Religion. The full-time Humanities teacher had resigned with only three years left before he qualified for retirement. He told the college administrator he was going to "meditate" in Puerto Rico. God allowed all the circumstances to be worked out in July, even before I knew I would need a job in August of the same year, 1978. I had a great chance to witness for my Lord to about forty students in this class that first semester. Many students in the first class were disappointed that their favorite teacher had resigned and were defensive when I shared my Christian testimony with them. I told them how the job came to be without my seeking, sharing my credentials as a born-again Christian, and having a degree that met the State of Florida's qualifications, which enabled me to hold the position that the Lord provided for me. By the end of the semester, I had earned the money for my husband's back treatments.

One night the Lord gave me a dream in which I saw the former teacher, whom I had never met or seen his picture, wandering in the wilderness. The next day in the World Religion class, I told the students about the dream and described the man I saw. They were amazed and said the former teacher looked just like the man in my dream. I told them how the Lord moved him to Puerto Rico so I could have his job, meet our financial needs, and be used as a witness in that setting.

God had another blessing for me and a plan to use me further. He gave us extra income as I was asked to teach Old Testament the next semester on the same campus. When I asked what text I was to use, the administrative assistant told me I could use any text I chose. I asked if I could teach from the Holy Bible.

The college representative said, "Since you are the instructor, choose whatever text you desire."

What a thrill to know I could teach on a secular campus and use the Word of God as a text! Other books were listed as requirements for outside reading from the previous semester, but I was given the freedom by God to teach primarily from His Word.

The Lord continued to pour out His grace by providing yet another semester to teach a class on the New Testament at Florida Junior College on the Kent Campus and World Religion at the Naval Air Station just a few miles down Highway 17. All my prayers were answered just as I had prayed. What a loving and faithful God we serve.

I prayed before each class, "Lord, have the students ask questions that will lead into an answer that only You can give." A most interesting event took place one day as a result of His answer to my prayer.

When I would have least expected it, in the middle of a Buddhism lecture, a student who had a Catholic background asked, "Mrs. McCormick, what does it mean to be 'born again'?"

The phrase had been used by President Jimmy Carter many times during interviews by the press. The students had opinions about what it meant, but some were confused. I had been cautioned not to take every occasion to share my Christian faith and to stick to the material at hand each day.

So with tongue in cheek, I asked, "Would you prefer I answer this question after class? I don't want to infringe on anyone's civil rights."

The heretic I loved, who sat in the back of the class and scoffed at Christianity spoke up, "Answer it now if you can!"

Others joined the rebel leader with various comments, wanting to hear what I would have to say.

My heart was full of excitement as I responded, "I can and I will."

What an open door! After I had explained in a simple and loving way, what the plan of salvation involved, the girl began to cry. I asked what experiences she had that had caused her pain regarding Christianity. She said she had been put-down by so-called "Christians" through the years because she was Catholic and associated pain with religious people.

She said, "I wish all Christians felt the way you do, Mrs. McCormick."

I explained what she experienced talking with me was because of God's real love in my heart for her. The class did not object to my answer or to my spirit because God had given me the opportunity I had asked for in class to show His love, concern, and plan for them all. They heard the truth and truth prevailed! I always prayed that when the doubting students heard the answers He sent, they would understand, be at peace, and satisfied that they had heard Truth as an absolute that could not be proven otherwise. A student who challenged me about truth asked if there was absolute truth. I said, "Absolutely!" I thought he might pass out pass out as his anger took over! He told me I could not know absolute truth. I told him he could not unless he knew Jesus who was Truth, the Way, and the Life. God gave me boldness to stand up for His Truth!

The Holy Spirit answered their needs for truth every time these situations came up. At the end of the course when I asked which religion we had studied answered life's questions, everyone, including the heretic and the disillusioned students who had been hurt by poor examples of professing believers, said only one... Christianity!

When I asked if Jesus through the Bible had provided the answers they sought, knowing most of them did not know the Bible doctrines or the Author, they could not say there was a problem with claims of Christ nor the Scriptures.

Though their eyes had been on those who were
inconsistent in living the Christian life
and they were skeptical of "church-goers,"
in Him was the Way, the Truth, and the Life revealed!

THE EMPTY NEST

We continued serving from 8,000 to 10,000 conferees each year as they came to the facility in Marianna for spiritual growth and fellowship. Other non-church groups also attended for planning sessions, training, and/or testing.

Michele finished school at Marianna High School and attended two years of college at Chipola College in Marianna, Florida. Using her speed typing skills, she then worked for the Jackson County School Board as secretary and learned much that would help her in other positions. When she moved to Jacksonville, Florida, in May of 1988, she work for the Florida Baptist Convention as secretary. Later, she worked as secretary and computer operator at General Business Services. Following that job she was hired to work with the City of Jacksonville Utilities Department by a former member of a Jacksonville church where David served as Minister of Music.

God continued to provide for her as she lived away from home. Michele enrolled in University of North Florida in Jacksonville, studying Business and Computers as she continued her job. She was engaged to Jerry Savery in November of 1989, while all the family was together for Thanksgiving in Pembroke, GA. Michele had always been interested in Jerry. Michael and the other youth in his church in Jacksonville respected him for the strong Christian stand he would take, even under opposition. David had gone to school with Jerry's aunt and years before had ridden the school bus that Jerry's grandparents drove. We had a strong connection with the family through the years.

The Lord worked all the details together for good in His time, bringing the two of them together.

Michael completed school at Marianna High School. He joined the U.S. Army and left for Boot Camp at Ft. Sill, Oklahoma, in September of 1988. After his thirteen weeks of Boot Camp and AIT (Advanced Training), he was given a choice of three-year assignment in Ft. Stewart, GA where his uncle worked as a civilian Music Consultant, or a chance for the two-year assignment overseas. He accepted the two-year assignment and after thirty days leave in December, he flew from Jacksonville, to Atlanta, to West Germany where he served in Kitzingen as well as in other parts of the country.

-66-

PROVISION IN THE STORM

While visiting in Michele's home in Jacksonville, I told her I wanted to get my hair cut by Sherri, a friend who cut my hair from time to time when I was in the city. She told me Sherri was working in a different shop located at Jacksonville Beach. Michele got the address from Sherri's mother-in-law and when I called Sherri to ask if she could cut my hair, she told me to come in the next few minutes and she would "work me in."

I left the house to drive to the beach although a storm was coming our way. The wind was blowing strongly and it began to rain. I began to wonder if a hurricane was on the way. Even with the windshield wipers on full force, I could hardly see the road as I drove. I prayed I would be able to see well enough to stay in my lane on the highway and that the Lord would help me find the address in the shopping center at the beach since I was not familiar with that area.

It was getting late in the day and I realized I had not eaten since breakfast. I asked the Lord to help me find a parking place in front of the beauty shop because of the bad weather and to provide a yogurt shop next door so I could get something to eat. The weather began to clear a bit as I approached the strip mall. I made a right turn and drove toward the beauty shop. There was a parking place in front of the shop and next door there was a yogurt shop! I thanked the Lord and rejoiced that He continued to care about all the things I needed. He also kept me safe in the storm. When I opened the door to the beauty shop, I told Sherri about what great things the Lord had done for me in that short span of time.

**The other beauty operators heard the testimony
and agreed with me that God had provided a miracle.**

Ask Yourself...

What amazing provision miracles from God have I experienced in my life?

How have these miracles influenced those in my sphere of influence?

Record these events in your journal and ask God to use you to influence others as you testify of His love and provision.

Read 1 Timothy 6:17.

What is God's promise to you concerning His provision?

How has this section changed the way you pray for your needs?

Part Ten
Dealing with the Powers
of Darkness

–67–

ENCOUNTER WITH THE SERPENT

One night when David was swimming alone in the pool at our house in Pompano Beach, FL he had his eyes shut and was relaxing when he opened his eyes to see a snake swimming toward him. I had cautioned him not to swim alone without the lights on in the pool area, but he enjoyed swimming in the dark. The snake was very close to his face and he began to panic! He swam as fast as he could, climbed out of the pool and ran in the house, dripping wet, calling for me to come in a hurry. We went back outside to see if the snake was still there. Then we called our neighbor over to see if he knew what kind of snake it was. He dipped a trash can down in the water and caught the snake. It was a deadly coral snake. The neighbor worked for the telephone company and told us he would be right back with his tools. He ran to his house, got the wire cutters and cut off the head of the snake. He reminded us that "red, black, yellow kill a fellow," a phrase we never forgot after that encounter.

Broken Fellowship

In 1979, while serving the church in Jacksonville, near Roosevelt Mall, we experienced confusion the devil can bring. There was trouble in the fellowship and people were at odds, one with the other. A well-meaning pastor had not included the congregation in making decisions in certain areas as he should. Problems had come to a head and a special business meeting was called. A department director from the Florida Baptist Convention was called in to be the moderator as the two factions were allowed to speak to the problems as they saw fit on a Wednesday night service. The result of the meeting was that the pastor was asked to resign. The majority of the congregation wanted David to stay as Minister of Music.

The same night, another church on the South side of Jacksonville, David's home church where his parents were members, was having a business meeting and voted to offer David a position on their staff as Minister of Music. The phone call came during the meeting asking him to accept the job. God provided a new work and a new ministry on a night when confusion seemed to prevail.

In the "fullness of time," God brought it all to pass.

-69-

EVIL SEEKS TO DESTROY

In David's home church, he found an ease in his work he had only known in one other church. The pastor and staff wanted to have me work also as a paid staff member. We had not been given that option in the other churches where David had served on staff. As happens so many times in church-related work, the wife works alongside the husband as a volunteer, even if she is qualified, trained, and educated for leadership on a paid basis. It appeared to be a good opportunity and yet something seemed to be clouding the issue. I felt the pastor was too eager to "put me on the staff." I was to be a part-time worker, but was hired full-time and paid a full-time salary. The job description was vague and the pastor began to change his mind as to what my duties were.

As I worked with the College & Career age group that grew in numbers, the pressure of not knowing what was expected of me by the pastor became hard to bear. Family problems arose and I felt torn between working and having proper emphasis on our home life. My mother had worked outside the home as my brother and I were growing up and I had always wanted her home with us. I told the Lord when we had children that I would stay home with them unless He brought jobs to me and I knew it was His will for me to work. He has sent every job I have had since that time.

All my support systems seemed to have been taken away during the dilemma I was facing and the devil began an all-out campaign to destroy me. I could not decide why I was a threat to him until the Lord showed me what an encouragement I had been to others in the church and how they had grown in Him. Many of the members of the church had become church leaders, due in part to God's encouragement through me. Then I learned something about emotional suffering and what it meant to be tried as by fire, becoming refined as gold. I held to those scripture verses as my strength.

Devil in the Hallway

One day, the devil showed up in a visual way. I saw his brownish gray shriveled face, just a head with no body, coming toward me, showing his teeth, as he came down the hallway in our home. I stood in my bedroom and held on to the bed-post. My body began to shake and uncontrollable tears came from my eyes.

I asked the Lord, "Am I going to have a nervous break-down or lose my mind?"

His Spirit spoke to my spirit immediately, from the opposite side of the room (I love that), high and lifted up, toward the ceiling, "No, you're mine!"

When He spoke, I felt peace flow into my spirit and realized my body was not shaking. I knew the devil must be gone. As I looked down the hallway, I saw him slowly fade away.

DEMON ON THE PHONE

As I was pondering what had just happened, I received a phone call from a church member my husband's family had known for many years. She was very charismatic and full of praise to the Lord, as a general rule and loved our family. I did not know that she was jealous that a friend of hers had not been given a paid position on the church staff, which she understood was promised to her by the pastor. Instead, I had been hired. I did not know she had these feelings until I received the phone call.

She made small talk for a short while and then a demonic voice began to take over her speech with horrible demonic words. I had seen excerpts in advertising the movie "The Exorcist" on television and realized the sound of her voice was just like the voice in the preview. My body began to tremble again and tears came from my eyes. All I could think to say was, "I forgive you in Jesus' name." I repeated this over and over as she spoke profanities and impurities. I knew the only defense I had against demonic warfare was the name of Jesus.

I had never had the forces of Hell surround me in this manner before, but I learned that it is very real. I knew the Lord would fight the battle and He would be victorious bringing me through the trial. It was hard to share my new testimony because so many people I talked with in my church had never experienced anything like this before. I told the Lord that I was willing to testify for Him concerning this experience and other victories He brought to pass in my life, but few people seemed to listen.

It was as though He spoke to my spirit and said, "You are telling the wrong people."

Most of the people I shared the experience with were members of the church. I knew He wanted me to share my testimonies with the lost. I found when I did this, they did listen and seeds of witness were planted in their lives.

DEMONIC ATTACK

In a church where David was on staff in South Florida, there was a man named Lawrence who had accepted Christ as Savior on a Sunday morning. He called me on the following Monday and asked me to come to his house. He said he and his wife were there with the devil who was trying to take his soul back. I asked my prayer partner to go with me into the unknown with the One who we knew would lead us and be our protector.

As we entered the home, we saw a man who looked like he was being torn apart mentally. His bushy, thin hair was almost standing on end. His eyes appeared to be glazed over. He told us to sit down. It appeared he was attempting to frighten us by telling us he had cast a spell on everyone in the church the night before, except for me. He said there was too much love around me and that was why he could not control me with a spell.

We talked to him about his salvation experience and quoted scriptures to help assure him he was saved. He asked the devil to leave his house and indicated he was kicking him out, as he walked to the open door and then closed it. Later, he took his wife to the bedroom and stayed there with her for a long while. My friend and I prayed for him during that time.

He came out of the room and talked with us in rambling phrases that were incoherent. He finally told us we could go home since he was feeling better. God's protection was with all of us that day. My friend and I were asked to minister, walking into the "unknown," but we knew the One who walked beside us.

The next week, Lawrence was put in a facility for the mentally disturbed. My husband and I went to see him twice while he was there, but could only speak to him through a window in his room's door that had bars over the glass. We never saw him again. He was soon moved to another facility to get further treatment.

Danger on the Highway

On one of my trips to take care of Mother for the weekend, the weather became foggy and rainy. On the last two hours of the trip, the visibility was impaired to the point I could hardly see the traffic on the road. Suddenly, I felt darkness around me like evil I could almost touch. At a crossroad not far from my hometown, I pulled out in the road to make a right turn but did not see a truck coming toward me in time to get out of the way. The driver hit me on the passenger side pushing me off the road. The van I was driving was totally destroyed. My glasses were knocked off my face and I could feel glass in my hair from the impact with the rear view mirror.

The highway patrol sent a car out within minutes. The black man who was driving the truck was not hurt badly, but we were both taken in the same ambulance to the nearest hospital. I could not fill out any of the paperwork because I did not have my glasses. I told the hospital personnel what to write down and gave them my insurance information. After I was checked out by a doctor, he dismissed me. I asked if I could see the man who hit me and find out his condition. He was in the same general area of the Emergency Room where I had been and his family had gathered around him. He and I talked for a few minutes and said we would pray for each other.

I made a phone call to my aunt who lived about forty miles away. She said she would send her son-in-law, my cousin's husband, to pick me up. He came in about thirty minutes and then we drove to the shop where the van had been taken by the wrecker company. We looked through the van in the dark, as best we could as I prayed we could find my glasses. I had also prayed that the right lens would be usable since I could see out of that eye better than the left. God answered my prayer. My cousin found the glasses. The left lens was crushed and the leg broken off on that side, but the right lens was still in what was left of the frames.

It was late when I arrived in my home town, so my mother and her caregiver were concerned that something must have happened to me. My brother and his wife came from Savannah when I called to let them know about the wreck. They were on their way to the mountains of North Georgia for a few days of vacation. They stopped by to see how I was and then continued on their trip. The caregiver left and I tried, as best I could to take care of Mother, at that point. I had multiple bruises and was very sore, but with the Lord's help, I was able to do what was necessary for Mother and me that weekend. David came to get me on Sunday and stopped by the Hinesville wrecker service to get some usable items out of the van.

I was kept from death once again by God's protection.

Ask Yourself…

What amazing events have I experienced that convince me God is watching over me even when the enemy tries to take me out?

Record these events in your journal and ask God to use you to influence others as you testify of His love and protection against the enemy's attacks.

Read 1 Peter 5:8.

What is God's promise to you concerning His protection against the attacks of the devil?

PART ELEVEN
FAMILY MIRACLES

-74-

FOUR CAR PILE UP

After picking Michael up at his kindergarten class held at our church, David and I bought groceries and filled the Chevy with gas. The weather was lovely, so we took the long way home, enjoying the ride. A vendor with a truck full of produce was set up on the right side of the highway, displaying a large sign listing products and prices. David was distracted and glanced toward the sign. The person driving his vehicle directly in front of us evidently was distracted also and came to a sudden stop. David did not respond in time to avoid hitting the car. The driver behind us could not stop in time and slammed into the rear of our vehicle. There was a chain reaction and the next car hit the one that damaged our car. Michael was in the back seat during this time and after the third impact, he reached for me as I reached for him, pulling him into the front seat.

As I held him close in my arms he said, "Let's get out of this car!"

In record time, a policeman arrived along with a fire truck and ambulance. The emergency responders told us not to get out of the car. The police officer conducted a preliminary investigation and the Emergency Medical personnel were then allowed to help us out of the car and check our vital signs. Several people who had been in the cars were lying on the ground being examined or were sitting on the grass waiting for first aid.

By God's grace, no one was seriously hurt.
As we looked at the four-car pileup, we could see
what a miracle it was people were doing well,
other than some emotional reactions.

Our big Chevrolet had been transformed into a compact car and looked as though there was no trunk area. A large pool of gasoline was under the car and could have easily caught fire at any moment. The firemen washed the fuel off the road and wrecker workers were standing by to move the vehicles out of the traffic jam.

We called our pastor, David's co-worker, and asked if he would come get us. When we got back to his house, we decided to bring Michael to the door in our arms and tell the pastor's wife that he was not doing well. We had already told them in the phone call that we were not injured, but Michael enjoyed playing a trick on her and it helped him feel like things were going to be all right. Comic relief helped him have a better day.

Since we did not have a functional vehicle at that point, the pastor and his wife told us we could use their Volkswagen as long as we needed it, since they had two cars. They were very gracious with their possessions and we thanked them for their giving spirit.

The Sunday that followed gave us the challenge of getting the four of us in the little "bug" and a neighbor's child who had begged to go to church with us. Her family was seldom home and were not good moral models for her. She spent a lot of time in the afternoons with us because she did not want to stay home alone. Her brother was gone most of the time with his friends, getting into mischief as a rule. The mother was working in a bar and the little girl rarely knew where her daddy was. The family German Shepard was her "baby sitter." When Sunday rolled around, the five of us squeezed into the small car, showed up for the church service with a story to tell of our weekend trials and how the Lord helped us overcome the dangers that were in our path.

-75-

LIFE SPARED

One day while David was busy working on the car, he called Michele out to help. She was only eight years old at the time. He told her to take the car out of park while he was working on something under the car. She was afraid to do what he said but afraid not to. I was working in the house, but he did not want to ask me to stop what I was doing to help him. I had no idea that he and Michele were involved in something so dangerous. When David told Michele he was ready for her to put the car in neutral, she pulled the gear shift down and the car began to roll backward, rolling over David. He yelled for her to put on the brakes and she did so but was terrified! They both came in the house very upset, telling me what had just happened. I could not believe they had been through something that could have had a terrible ending.

**We thanked God for his watchful care and protection
as they came near "the valley and shadow of death."**

MEAT

One of my "every-day miracles" happened on a day I had bought groceries. We did not have the money to buy meat and get the other things we needed for the family. I told David I could not buy meat. My son went with me across the street to make our purchases for the family. I explained to him why we could not buy meat. We bought the groceries we could afford and walked back home, unloaded the groceries, and then went out to play ball in the backyard.

A neighbor who watched us go and come from place to place each week, whether to the store or church as a family, was sitting in her yard that day with her cat. She came over to where we were playing. While we talked, she asked if we would like some de-boned chicken breasts, saying she had a supply in her freezer, individually wrapped, that she could not use. That sounded to me like the Lord was providing meat for my table. It was not logical that a lady who lived alone could not use de-boned chicken breasts, individually wrapped, which was perfect for her use! I am sure God prompted her to give the chicken to our family, on the very day I could not afford to buy meat!

We did not have to buy meat that day because the Lord already had a plan to provide it.

Miracles come into my life often. I know the source and in our children's teachable years, I pointed out where they came from. When these miracles occurred, I asked Michele and Michael what the source of the blessing was and they would say, "Jesus." It was so obvious! The Lord loves to meet our needs and reward our faith. He knows I will give Him praise and all the credit for the blessing and share the news with those who will listen. What a joy to teach our children these lessons in the everyday circumstances He sends!

EASTER EGGS

Michael came home from school one afternoon saying he needed to bring a dozen eggs to school the next day for an Easter egg hunt. David was out of town and I had no money nor did I have a vehicle. The store was several blocks away from the house. I looked through my billfold and Michael looked in his piggy bank for coins. All we could find was seventy cents. Eggs at that time were ninety cents a dozen. I told him the Lord knew what we needed for school the next day and we would go to the store in faith, believing God would provide the twenty cents we needed to pay for the eggs. He and I walked all the way to the little store, looking for lost coins along the road. I told him to help me look around outside the store, before we went inside, to see if we could find twenty cents that someone may have dropped on the ground. We found one dime. I was excited and asked him if he saw what the Lord had provided. He said, "Yes," and was excited, too, but we still needed one more dime.

We had not noticed a black man standing nearby using an outside pay telephone. Hearing the conversation, he came over to where we were standing and said he was impressed to give us a dime. I thanked him and told him God had given us the dime through him. He was a Christian and agreed God had provided. I asked Michael who gave us the dime. He said, "Jesus." It was a wonderful lesson he learned. We exercised our faith and it was stretched to another level.

We went in the store, bought the eggs, and walked back home together. What a wonderful memory the Lord made possible! Some people see these situations as problems. Some say we should not bother God with what they consider trivial matters. We saw an opportunity for the Lord to come down and meet our little needs as well as the big ones. He cares about everything that concerns us.

I have learned that He wants to help us with all our concerns so we can keep our minds on Him and give Him the glory for each good and perfect gift.

MIRACLE ON HALLOWEEN 1977

When Michael was in second grade, he was going to bed and getting ready for our prayer time. With tears in his eyes, he said, "Mama, I'm the only one in our family who is not a Christian. I feel Jesus knocking at my heart's door."

I asked him how he would like to respond and he said, "Open the door and let Jesus come in."

On the wall in his bedroom was the famous painting of Jesus knocking on the door. The artist painted the door with no doorknob on the outside. Many sermons have been preached concerning the need for the one on the inside to open the door and let Jesus in. God used many influences through the years to reach Michael heart's door. I believe He even used the picture of Jesus on the wall of his bedroom.

I explained how he could be saved. He prayed and asked Jesus to take his sins away and come live in his heart. Jesus gave him the desire to be saved and the ability to respond to Him in faith, as a little child. We talked about what the experience meant. He was happy that at last because now we were all Christians.

What a special Halloween that was for us. It was a holiday we did not "celebrate" as a family for several reasons, one being Michele's fear of anyone in a costume and mask. I usually played games with Michele and Michael around the house, turning off lights and having fun in the dark. We pretended we were not home, so no one would come to the door and scare Michele.

This Halloween, while some folks were out taking part in "things of the night" our son had been saved by the Lord Jesus!

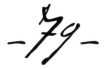

The Chair 1977

While we were renting the house from the bookkeeper of the church where David was Minister of Music, I told him we needed to have an old chair recovered. When David and I got married, my mother had given me the chair that had been in my home when I was growing up. We used it for another nine years. The money was not available for us to pay to have the chair covered, but I prayed about it and left the matter in the Lord's hands.

About a week later, one of our friends from our church in Jacksonville, came to see me. She and her husband had a tight budget but were good stewards of what God had given them. The family of four was thrifty and my friend had craft skills and had made various items to furnish their home. She asked me if I knew of anyone who had a chair she could use to cover in a class she was taking in upholstery. That week she had signed up to take the class and the first assignment was covering a chair. I told her my chair that needed to be recovered and about my prayer for the Lord to help me get it done as economically as possible.

She and I were so pleased that the Lord had worked out our needs perfectly.

All she needed me to do was furnish the chair and the material with which to cover it. I asked her what kind of material was best for me to buy for the project. She took measurements of the chair, told me how many yards of material to get and suggested I buy nylon because it was durable and easy to sew.

I went to Cloth World and prayed the Lord would help me find a remnant of nylon material the right length, rose in color, and width at a good price. As I walked in the store I saw the word "Remnants" on a sign posted over a vat of materials. Almost immediately I saw a rose-colored nylon piece of fabric, measured it and realized it was more than I needed. My friend used the extra material to make me a footstool I had wanted. God is so good to give us more than we ask when we give Him all the praise!

SUICIDE ATTEMPT

David's mother, Willie McCormick, went through a period of depression while still living in Jacksonville, but his dad had not let us know about the problem. They had planned to visit us in Marianna and his daddy thought he would discuss the situation with us at that time. We could tell something was wrong when we saw her but did not know to what extent. As I spent time with her, I realized she was saying she wanted to die. She sat and rocked herself back and forth telling me she was very confused. Her eyes were glassy in appearance. She seemed to be afraid. I asked what she was afraid of and she could not tell me.

A day or two later, I told David that I knew that his mother wanted to die and he and his daddy should watch her closely. They did not think it was that serious, but having been through my daddy's suicide, I knew to listen carefully when someone let you know they were thinking of taking their life. It was a way of crying out for help and was not to be dismissed. His daddy reluctantly told us, as he was driving from Jacksonville to Marianna, his wife had told him to drive off the road so they both would be killed together.

The First Baptist Choir Christmas party was held at Blue Springs Baptist Assembly one night while his folks were still staying in the guest room downstairs near the office area. His mother did not want to eat with the group, so we brought their meal to their room that night. The next night we were taking the bell choir from First Baptist Church to Dothan, Alabama, to play a program of Christmas music at the mall. David, Michele, and I were involved in the bell choir program. Michael had plans to go to a Christmas party for his age group. David's daddy said he thought he and Willie would be fine alone at the assembly.

Willie took her bath first that night. When his daddy went into the bathroom to take his bath, he did not know she had taken a bottle of pills and swallowed them one at a time, until she had taken them all. When his daddy came out of the bathroom, she told him what she had done. If she had wanted to die, I don't believe she would have told him from what I have read concerning folks who are suicidal. His daddy tried to keep her from going to sleep and began calling the upstairs apartment phone to see if anyone had come home yet.

Michele road back from Dothan with some of the bell ringers and got back home before we did. Michael came home from his party about the time Michele did. David and I had to go by First Baptist Church to put up the bells, the cases, the music, and music stands. Michele and Michael heard their granddaddy calling their names from downstairs. They ran down to see what was wrong. They put their grandmother in the car and Michele was told to drive by her granddaddy. Michael was told to keep his grandmother awake any way he could. It was hard on both of them to have to be in this situation. Michele was crying and could hardly see how to drive as they rushed toward the local hospital.

When they arrived in the emergency room, the hospital personnel began working on Willie, placing a tube down her throat as they administered charcoal. Dennis, our Minister of Music from First Baptist Church who had been with us in Dothan got back to town before we did. When he heard what had happened, he went to our apartment to wait for us and take us to the hospital. This was in the days before cell phones. Dennis kept calling the music suite phone in hopes we would hear it. As we finished putting up all the bell equipment, we finally heard the phone and Dennis told us what had happened. We left the church immediately and met him at the hospital.

David's mother was doing better by the time we arrived and we all talked with her. She was kept in the hospital for several days. Then David's daddy took her back to Jacksonville where his mother was put in the hospital on the psychiatric ward for observation and therapy. After several weeks of being in the hospital, she returned home with medication to take and a program of prescribed exercises to do daily.

It took quite some time before she got back to normal, but again the Lord intervened and a life was saved.

-81-

DANGEROUS MISTAKE 1990

As I began to wake up one morning, I was filled with a strong sense of God's grace and special care for me. I made my bed, dressed, and headed for the kitchen for my "muffin and hot tea" routine. Thinking of the minor pain in my joints and my vinegar plus honey treatment, I reached down underneath the kitchen sink and picked an unlabeled gallon jug. By mistake, I had picked up a container of industrial strength bleach that was next to the vinegar. The industrial bleach used at the assembly was much stronger than bleach sold for home use. I had never made this mistake before. For some reason, I decided not to mix the vinegar with honey as I usually did and planned to take each item separately. I poured out about three tablespoons of bleach in a cup and drank it. At once, I realized it did not taste like vinegar and knew it was bleach! I drank about eight glasses of water as quickly as I could. My heart was pounding!

I tried to use the walkie-talkie radio in my kitchen knowing that it did not always have good coverage, but hoped to contact my husband who was working in the assembly youth camp about a mile away. Miracle of miracles, he heard my transmission and answered me! I asked that he come home if possible. It was not a good time for him to leave his duties there, but after I explained how serious my situation was, within minutes he was in the apartment. By that time, I had called the local hospital to ask the representative for advice. I had confidence that I would be fine.

**I knew the Lord was watching over me and
would not allow Satan to destroy me.**

The hospital clerk who answered the phone gave me an 800 number to call. The lady who answered that call asked what kind of bleach I drank. When I told her it was industrial strength, she was very concerned and asked for the details concerning the product. My husband called Jerry, the maintenance man at the assembly, to get the information from him. Jerry was able to get the transmission, which was another miracle, and told David that the concentration was 12.5 water to one part bleach. The poison control representative said that was "a bit high." We told her I had drank eight glasses of water immediately when I realized I drank bleach. She said to drink a pint of milk. We were out of milk at the apartment, so David had to drive two miles to the youth camp, get milk, and bring it back to me. We thanked the lady at poison control for her help when we called back to report I drank the milk. She said she would call later and check on me. I still felt nervous but was still confident that I was in the Lord's hands and no harm would come to me. I drank more milk later in the afternoon.

I had read my Bible around 7:30 A.M. and knew the scripture was appropriate for the day's events. I hurried back to my Living Word to re-read the portion of scripture I had read when I first got up. The passage was Deuteronomy 4:4 which said, "You who did cleave unto the Lord your God are alive, every one of you this day."

**I was alive because "greater is He that is in me than he that is
in the world."**

-82-

MICHAEL'S WRECK 1991

We were working in the Youth Camp kitchen when I received a call from one of Michael's friends, saying he had just been in a wreck but was okay. David had been working in the office that morning at the Adult Assembly and I was helping in the Youth Camp. He said he would go see about Michael and I should stay by the phone since he and I were the only office workers.

Someone had pulled out from the North, at an intersection by the new Oak Station mall on Highway 90, two miles from the assembly. Traffic was flowing both east and west and it was raining. When the driver of the car pulled out in front of Michael, he suddenly put on breaks. Michael looked over into the left lane and saw two friends of his in another vehicle. In order not to hit the car in front of him or his friends in the car next to him, he pulled to the left as far as he could and headed for the median. A witness told us his Jeep began to spin around and flipped over on the driver's side causing his right leg to be forced out of the right window.

A man from the tire company on the right side of the road saw the accident and thought Michael must have been killed. He ran over to the site. By that time, Michael said he heard a lady praying for him to be okay and asking God to spare his life. He looked around and saw no one. He thought about the possibility that it was me or our head cook and good friend, Vera, a lady of prayer who loved the Lord. He did not see the lady nearby and the man from the tire company did not see anyone either. Perhaps it was an angel hovering over him, sent to protect him from harm.

The man saw Michael was okay and although he asked Michael to stay still, he insisted that he wanted to stand up due to the pain in his leg. His hip was hurting pretty bad where he had landed on it. David arrived and gave Police Officer Peters the insurance information he needed. Michael was then taken to the hospital and checked for injuries.

He was fine through a miracle of the Lord!

The Jeep had plastic windows and gave little protection. No one was hurt in any other cars involved. The person who pulled out on the highway, causing the problem, was nowhere to be found.

A few weeks after the accident, a traffic light that had been needed since the mall opened was put up at that intersection. Michael had wanted to have the Jeep painted ever since he bought it. He paid cash for the vehicle when he first got home from Desert Storm but did not have enough money for the paint job. After the wreck, he was blessed with the money from the insurance company to get the jeep painted.

BUDDY'S MIRACLE JOB

Buddy had become a popular guitar player at Ft. Stewart Army Base near Savannah where he had the opportunity to play for several events over a period of time. Although he was not a civil service employee, miraculously he had been chosen by General Norman Schwarzkopf, General of the Army Base, to be Manager of the Music Building and the planning of Armed Forces Variety Shows. This job enabled him to have insurance for the first time, to cover him and his wife. The work was hard. He had long hours and after the performances had to clean the floors of the auditorium where the shows were held. This was difficult for him due to his back problems resulting from the way he had to walk with the brace he wore from his hip to his ankle. He did an excellent job and was voted Handicapped Man of the Year during his time of employment there, as well as helping the soldiers win an award for the best variety show for all the Army bases in the USA!

WRECK NEAR ARMY BASE

After getting off work one day and closing the Music Center at Ft. Stewart Army Base, Hinesville, GA, my brother was on his way home to Savannah as it began raining heavily. His van hit a pocket of water and hydroplaned, landing off the left shoulder of the road and rolling down an embankment. The van was totaled. His guitar, amplifier, and other items of equipment were being thrown through the van. When the van stopped, Buddy realized the top of the vehicle had been ripped open and his hand was severely cut by the torn metal. He had other injuries and a lot of blood was pouring from his head.

The Lord was watching over him.

Some soldiers were right behind him on the road and saw the wreck occur. They had stretchers and first aid materials in the military trucks. Six of them surrounded him and checked out his injuries. Buddy used this as a chance to witness. He wiped off the blood from his face and told the young men he was okay. He asked them if they knew the Lord Jesus as their Savior. He told them even if he died, he was safe in the Lord because he had trusted his soul to Jesus. Even though he is right-handed he said, "Thank God, it is my right hand. I can still make a living playing chords with my left hand and strum with my right!"

He had several hand surgeries in the following months. Some of the tendons could not be saved and were thrown in the trash. Buddy had limited usage of his right hand but was still able to strum the guitar and continue entertaining in restaurants where he played dinner music making a living. The insurance money he received replaced his van and he and his wife were able to get another vehicle for her to drive. Out of the bad situation, their needs were met and it turned out to be a blessing.

Through the suffering, they had another chapter to add to their testimony of God's goodness.

-85-

WRECK IN MARCH 1994

Michele, David, and I were supposed to play handbells in our friend Amy's wedding at 4 P.M. Michele and Jerry had come from Jacksonville the night before and were to return Saturday night. Jerry was at the apartment at the assembly reading. We went to the church to practice with the other bell ringers. David had scored the music for the wedding. The rehearsal did not go as well as he had hoped. Two of the clip-on lamps that were attached to the top of the music folders had fallen from the table in the balcony where our bells were set up and landed on the pews below. Changes had to be made in the length of the pieces. After about two hours of practice, the group was prepared to play for the wedding, so we left the church and started back to the assembly.

Jerry and Michele had recently purchased a 1991 white, four-door Plymouth and made one payment on the vehicle she was driving that day. David had ridden in the front seat on the way to the church. On the way home, she wanted me to sit in the front seat, so David sat in the back. We saw a friend of Michele's in the lane next to us as we were about two miles from the assembly. As we approached the Oak Station shopping center, Michele and the friend waved to each other as we passed his car. When we reached the intersection in front of the shopping center, a lady named Mrs. Davis, traveling west, slowed and then turned South, at the light, to pull in to the shopping mall entrance. She evidently did not see our car because she pulled into our path. There was nowhere to go. Michele tried to turn as far to the right as she could to avoid the collision, but she could not get out of the way of the vehicle. Mrs.

Davis's car hit the front left of Michele's car, throwing the back left of the car into Mrs. Davis's car for the second impact, hurling Michele's car into a truck facing North.

The driver of the truck, Mr. McNeill, saw the car coming toward his vehicle and tried to put his gear shift into reverse to lessen the impact, but instead shifted into "PARK!" After the third impact, the car stopped. David was thrown to the left side of the car and had a bruised shoulder and a cut on his ear. He was able to get out of the car, although he was sick at his stomach for a few minutes. The driver's air bag inflated and saved Michele from serious injuries. Her left hand was cut in several places and glass was impacted in her wounds. Her arm also had a cut. A few weeks later when she went to the doctor, she realized she had a break just below her little finger on her left hand. Her knee was bruised and she had a lump on her head.

I had four broken ribs on the left side and a bruised hip and my spine was pushed over to the right. Emergency personnel were called as we waited for assistance. David called Jerry and let him know about the accident. Our son was out with his girlfriend. We did not have cell phones, so we could not reach him. The passenger in the truck, a very thoughtful young man named Tracey, watched over me as we waited for the emergency vehicle to arrive. He had noticed I was having trouble breathing.

The 911 attendants arrived a short time later. David and I did not know Tracey, but Michele did. He was stationed in Jacksonville at the Naval Air Station, had been in Desert Storm, as Michael had been, and was in school when Michael attended Marianna High School. I had taught World Religion at the Naval Air Station during the 1970's, so we had a few things in common. We talked briefly as he kept watch over me. The 911 personnel, Mr. Willis, Mr. Owens, and Mr. Pierce arrived and placed Michele and me in the same ambulance. It was interesting that we had names in common, my maiden name being Owens. Mr. Willis was married to the secretary who worked at the Christian school that met on the BSBA grounds that we managed, so he knew us.

Corporal Cox, the policeman who investigated the accident, was gentle and professional as he asked his questions. He cited Michele for not wearing her seat belt. We wrote his superiors and told them how impressed we were with his concern for us and his efficiency. We heard on the dispatch radio that four cars and an eighteen-wheeler truck had been in an accident on Interstate 10, just about three miles from our wreck. I prayed for those involved in that crash, while we were on our way to the hospital. When I saw a state patrolman come into the Emergency Room where I was being examined, I asked about the condition of the people who were involved in the accident on I-10 and Highway 71. He said it was not as bad as it was first reported. I told him I had prayed that would be the case. He was pleased to know there had been prayer for those folks.

Later the same day, we heard a church member's daughter was in another accident. She had hit a deer that ran out in front of her car. She was not hurt, but a lot of damage was done to her car.

God was protecting us all that day.

The ride to the hospital was rough and I continued to have problems breathing. Michele was quite upset and felt responsible for getting us all hurt. I tried to help her not feel guilty and be calm. We were taken to different areas in the Emergency Room and assistants began checking our injuries. We were sent to X-ray. Mark, our Minister of Music, stayed with me while the X-rays were being made. Jerry arrived at the hospital about that time as well as our friend, Lowell, the father of the bride. I told the attendance I could hear my friend's voice. He stopped in the hallway just for a moment to see me. I remember trying to assure him all was well regardless of the pain by saying, "The Lord is good." Pain pills were prescribed by the doctor on duty and we were all dismissed.

Many people ask, "Why did this happened to me?"

When things go "wrong," they judge events in their lives. I usually think it is better to ask why so many good things happen to us daily and we are spared so many tragedies. After all, God showers good things on us every day.

Jerry had driven our van to the hospital. He helped Michele to the van and David tried to help me. I could tell I was too weak to stand. A hospital attendant sat me down and checked my blood pressure. It was 77/44. He told David I could not go home until the blood pressure was at a safe level. When Michael and Christy got back to the assembly, they found a note at our apartment that Jerry had written concerning the wreck. They stayed with me once they got to the hospital. David and Michele left and I rested until my blood pressure improved. About thirty minutes later and after being given two pain pills, I was dismissed with two prescriptions. We went to the pharmacy and got the prescriptions for the pain medication and swelling in the rib cage.

Other than the pain and discomfort, it was like having a family reunion that day. Rebecca, a friend of Michele's, had come out to the assembly to see how we were and started making sandwiches for us since we had missed lunch. The wreck was the topic of conversation as we pieced together the events we remembered. Michele and Jerry wanted to go back to Jacksonville, get her prescriptions filled at the Jacksonville drug store they normally used, and try to get things settled at home. I got in the tub for a bath and David took a shower. He left me in the tub and ran an errand on the assembly grounds. He told he would be back to help me get out of the tub, but after waiting quite some time, I asked the Lord to help me get out. I have no idea how He did it, but I was able to get out with much pain and effort. I dried off, got dressed, and found a place to recline in a lounge chair in the living room where I could sit by the phone and take the business calls for the assembly.

When the accident reports came in a week or so later, we realized how much damage was done to the car and how fortunate we were that God was again watching over us. Mrs. Davis' car sustained $4,000 worth of damages, Mr. McNeill's truck had $1,000 worth of damages, and Michele's car was totaled with over $10,000 worth of damages. She and Jerry were disappointed about the loss of the car because they considered it the best vehicle they had ever had and they enjoyed driving it so much.

Mrs. Minchew, Ms. Baker, Mr. Melvin, and Mr. Ben were all witnesses to the collision. Mr. Ben was Michele's friend who had just spoken to us as we passed by his car prior to the collision. I was interested in which of my prayer cards Mrs. Minchew's name was on since I prayed daily for the church members whose last name started with "M" as mine did. The accident happened on Saturday and Mrs. Minchew's name appeared on the Saturday card! There were angels all around that day and a lady I prayed for was a witness in our behalf.

These things do not just happen.
They are God-ordained for those who trust in Him as their
provider and sustainer!

The handbell clinician, Christine Anderson, who was considered by many in the church music world to be the best handbell player in the USA, was finishing a conference at BSBA that same Saturday and spending the night in order to play handbells the next day at First Baptist Church where we were members. I realized she could play the handbells in our place since Michele and I could not go to the wedding later that day. David had decided he would go to the service and just sit in the balcony and oversee "his" bell choir playing "his" arrangements. Our Minister of Music's wife, Lisa, an excellent pianist, and Renee, a member of the bell choir, filled in for us and played our assigned bells. Christine agreed to play the bell music for the wedding and after a short rehearsal with the other ladies, was ready to present the lovely wedding music with our local musicians.

**How amazingly God worked it all out in advance
and "all things did work together for good" as
He has promised.**

David's folks had moved from Jacksonville due to health problems in 1992 and lived in the trailer park purchased by the Florida Baptist Convention a short time before. We were the landlords and had the responsibility of the trailer park property in addition to being overseers of Blue Springs Baptist Assembly. On Sunday, the day after our wreck, David's eighty-four-year-old mother was taken to the Emergency Room with pain in her ribs. She had fallen the same day as our wreck but did not want to let us know because of our emergency. Her pain got worse on Sunday and she knew she had to see a doctor. Her X-ray showed that she had a broken rib. She was put in a brace for support and adjusted to the situation well. In fact, she seemed to have more to say about her other on-going health problems. We could not believe we both had broken our ribs on the same day but we're grateful that the conditions were not more serious.

God covered us all with His protection.

Michael's Miracles in the Military

Many miracles happened to Michael while he was in the Army. During his basic training, a battle buddy panicked one day when he and Michael were learning how to pull the pin in the hand grenade and throw it in a matter of seconds. Michael had pulled the pin in his grenade and thrown it to a safe area. The battle buddy had pulled the pin and dropped his grenade. Michael jumped out of the fox hole and the sergeant on duty jumped in the hole, grabbed the grenade, and threw it just before it went off. Michael, the battle buddy, and the sergeant could have been injured or killed, but God protected them. The battle buddy was punished for putting them all in danger.

Michael was kept from danger as he made parachute jumps at night while stationed in Germany. Not being able to see and having to judge how close he was to the ground, Michael hurt his ankle once or twice but was not seriously injured.

One night during military maneuvers in Germany, Michael was assigned the task of guiding a tank into position while walking behind it with light beams he had in his hands. When they reached the designated area, Michael gave the signal to STOP. The driver did not stop. Michael realized he was going to be run over. He hit the ground and rolled into a low area the Lord had provided to keep him safe. The tank ran over him, but he was not touched.

**God's miracles continued to cover him as we asked
that he be covered daily.**

I had been praying for Michael one particular day, to be aware
of danger around him. I was not sure why I was led to pray that way,
but I knew he usually was very aware of his surroundings. This
seemed to be a specific need that I should pray for. When Michael
got home, I asked him if he could remember a need like that. He
said it must have been the night he and his battle buddy were out
wearing night-vision goggles and suddenly he was aware of danger
off to his right. He turned and there was a desert cobra raising up
its head. He did not tell me how he got away from the danger, but I
had a good idea what had happened. The important thing was God
prompted me to pray and answered my prayer providing once again
miracles with Michael's name on them.

One morning in the desert, Michael and his buddy were assigned
to go out on patrol in a tank. They were assured no enemy forces
had been seen that day. When they reached their destination, they
got out the binoculars and there before them was the Republican
Guard in force. We did not hear the rest of the story but know God
took care of both he and his friend once again.

We had prayed he was safe in the arms of the Lord.

Michael returned home May 22, 1991, from Desert Storm, the
same day our National Guard Unit returned. David and I went
to Tallahassee to meet him. His schedule had been changed after
he talked with us by phone and his plane arrived earlier than we
had been told it would. He was the only soldier we saw when we
entered the airport. It was so good to hold him once again. We took
him out to supper and talked with him as he brought up subjects

he wanted to talk about. There was much he did not want to share from the horrors he had experienced.

When we got home, he walked through the apartment at Blue Springs Baptist Assembly and to his room. He just looked at everything as though he could hardly believe he was home. Then he went to the refrigerator and opened it. He just stood there for a few minutes as we watched. He told us he could not imagine just being able to eat anytime he wanted to. The food had run short in his unit because of all the Iraqis that surrendered instead of choosing to fight and his unit fed their "prisoners of war." When he and his buddies came through Iraq toward the end of the war, he had very little food and water left. He saw the people begging for food and gave his food to the little girls who touched his heart. We don't know what he ate after that time or when.

I had prayed during the war that Michael would not be harmed nor anyone in his unit. When he came home, I asked him if he knew of any of the soldiers in his unit being harmed. He said he did not of any. What a miracle they were able to come home safely! As we talked, I asked Michael if he felt he was safe having been used to being on guard for so long. He said he did not feel safe. For months after arriving home, he was always checking things out to make sure he was secure.

While Michael was out with some friends one night, he was injured trying to help one of the guys who was attacked by several other young men. Michael's head hit a concrete curb and he was bleeding badly. He could have been killed, but the Lord spared him again. He made it through Desert Storm, yet when he was back home he was still not out of danger. He could have lost his life in two car wrecks months apart and this dangerous fall.

**He came through all these experiences as
God took care of him.**

-87-

EMOTIONAL FAMILY CRISIS

Late one night, my cousin, Harry, called late at night to tell me his wife, Jenny, was having continued emotional problems and the situation was to the point that she needed to be in a facility where she could get treatment. There were two loaded guns in the house and a few months before Jenny had taken an overdose of sleeping pills. It was an uncertain situation that I was walking into, but I knew God would protect me and work things together for good. Harry needed me to come be with him and do what I could to help with the situation. I told him I would pray about it and see what the Lord wanted me to do. I drove six hours to South Georgia the next day to be with him.

When I arrived at their home, there were two neighbors visiting the family. One of ladies was in the bedroom helping Jenny pack items that she would need while in the hospital that was located about eighty miles away. Jenny seemed upset in her unstable state of mind and was not pleased that I was in her house. When I arrived she asked me why I was there and I told her Harry had asked me to come. She did not say anything to me later when she came through the living room where I was talking with Harry. He asked me to pray that the Lord would work out a way for them to pay for the stay in the hospital since they did not have insurance coverage at that time.

He and I prayed. A few minutes later Jenny's psychiatrist, Dr. Harold, called to let him know that he had called the hospital and Jenny could have treatment for $100.00. Harry asked if he meant $100.00 a day. The doctor said, "No, just $100.00, as long as she wants to stay." Harry and I thanked the Lord for the miracle of answered prayer.

Then he asked me to pray with him that Jenny would agree to be checked in to the hospital without resistance. After Jenny packed and unpacked for about an hour, unable to make decisions even with a friend's help, she was ready to go but was concerned about the cost for her treatment. We all gathered at the front door of the house to start on our trip. Jenny agreed that she would go to the hospital when Harry told her how the Lord had worked out the financial details. As we started to walk out the door, she turned and told me that I was not going. She was very upset that I assumed I was going to be allowed to go with her. I told Harry that I had thought I was there to help her, but I realized I was sent to support him, so I agreed to stay at their house and wait for him to return.

The group left in two vehicles about 6:00 P.M. When they arrived at the hospital, Jenny wanted to have the keys to her car. Then she drove away leaving the group standing in front of the hospital. They did not know where she was going nor what she would do. There was a bridge nearby and they became concerned that she might drive off the bridge and take her life. In about thirty minutes, she came back to the hospital and told Harry she was ready to be checked in. He returned home about midnight and told me what had happened. She was in the facility about a week going through treatment until she convinced the doctors that she was fine and ready to go back home. We had hoped she would stay long enough to get her medicines regulated and her emotions would be under control, but she would not stay any longer.

As I looked back, I could see the miracle of God as He watched over us in a tense situation that could have turned in to a tragedy. She and Harry had loaded guns in their bedrooms. He was sure she would not resort to using the weapons on herself or anyone else, but the potential was there for a tragedy.

We trusted in the Lord for His protection and watch care and He kept us from harm.

FALLEN TREE

One night in June 2011, there was a storm in the area where I live. There was lightning, thunder, and high winds. As I lay down in my bed around 10:00 o'clock, I could hear the hickory nuts and pine cones hitting the deck outside my bedroom window, sounding like I was under attack by a foreign power! After I read a chapter in my Bible, I covered up and drifted off to sleep. The next day, I saw the deck was covered with small limbs, pine cones, and debris. After breakfast, I drove out of my garage to head toward town to run some errands. That was when I noticed about half of a large oak tree had fallen near the driveway. I got out of the van to see if a possible lightning strike caused the damage. It was difficult for me to determine what had caused the tree to fall. What a blessing to realize the tree did not fall in the driveway nor on the house! The tree fell in a perfect place, in the tree bed where limbs rested just at the edge of driveway.

A few days later, the man who did my lawn care cut up the tree limbs and cleaned off the grounds around the fallen tree. He told me he thought the tree fell because termites had eaten through the limbs and weaken the tree. When the strong winds blew through my property during the storm, the tree split in half and down it came! It could have fallen any day when I was outside walking to my mailbox. I could have been injured or perhaps lost my life.

God protected me from this possibility.

-89-

THE ELECTRICAL SYSTEM

November 26, 2011, I left Jacksonville after spending Thanksgiving holidays with my family. I stopped to get gas before driving to Kissimmee, Florida, for a vacation at our timeshare. When I cranked the van, I realized my navigation system, radio/CD player, windshield wipers, AC, and power windows were not functioning. However, the power steering, brakes, and the panel showing gas gage were useable, so I could drive safely. As I drove the problem continued for over two hours. The temperature in the van increased, but there was no way for me to get any cool air. I prayed for the Lord to lead me to the right dealership when I arrived in the Orlando area where I could get necessary repairs at a reasonable cost. My second prayer was that God would "heal" the system for His own glory and for His pleasure.

Stopping at a convenience store for a break, I parked the van and continued to pray for God to show me what He planned to do, knowing all things were in His hands. When I got back in the van a few minutes later, I cranked the van and all systems were restored! I was so excited. I thanked God over and over, praising Him for His care for me and my concerns. In my spirit, I was impressed to thank God for yet another miracle to write in my book.

When I went home about a week later, I took the van into the Chrysler dealership for the 3,000-mile service and asked that the mechanic check out the "new" problem I had experienced on my trip to South Florida. There was a theory that the cause of the system failure involved the ignition switch.

**It was a wonderful time for me to share my story
and give credit to God for taking care of all my needs.**

-90-

GRADUATION AND THE WEATHER

In January 2013, after lifting too many heavy loads while in the mountain house in Blairsville, GA, my back pain increased so that I could hardly walk. The regular monthly chiropractic treatments I have had for over thirty years were increased to twice a week for two months when I got back home to Marianna. Due to the pain, I tried to stay home during that time and take care of the back and hip as best I could, not making any trips more than an hour or so away, one being the Friday night in April when I sang with the Florida Worship Choir at First Baptist Church in Panama City.

My first trip after the injury in January was on Wednesday, June 5, 2013, when I drove to Jacksonville, FL to be in town for my grandson, Kyle's, High School graduation. There was some rain as I traveled on Interstate 10, but the weather was clear for most of the journey. When I arrived in Jacksonville, my son-in-law told me a bad storm was heading toward Jacksonville. That night, we went out with the family and extended family to eat, celebrating my grandson's graduation and his cousin's graduation. It rained most of the evening.

My son-in-law's mother had some heart problems while we were having our meal together and one of the relatives who was in our party, an employee of Mayo Clinic, assessed the situation and called 911 to have her taken to the hospital by EMS. After her vital signs were taken and tests run, it was found that she had a heart rate of 42. The week before, she'd had a doctor's appointment and was told she was doing well. Our prayers were with her as she stayed overnight at the hospital Wednesday night. The next day,

June 6, she asked if she could go to graduation. The doctor said she could, so she joined the family members at the Civic Center for the Sandalwood High School graduation. The showers were coming down as we entered the building. I prayed the rain would slack by the time we left the graduation. When we came out there was just a drizzle. About twelve of us went out to eat and had a wonderful time celebrating. That night I prayed the weather would improve so I could safely drive to South Georgia to see my son the next day. He and his wife did not get off work in time to eat with us on Wednesday night but did meet at the restaurant for a short visit.

Jerry, my son-in-law, told me he really did not want to see me go to South Georgia on Friday because the force of the storm was going to hit the North Florida/South Georgia area. I told him I was going to pray that the Lord would send the storm out to sea so it would do no damage and my path would be clear. Before we went to bed, we watched the weather report and saw the map covered with the rain pattern. As I lay down to sleep, I prayed again that the Lord would grant my request, just for His own good pleasure, and send the storm out to sea to protect people in our area. While praying the prayer, I could see in my mind's eye the Lord standing in the boat with the disciples on the sea of Galilee saying to the winds and waves, "Peace, be still." I thanked Him for the confirmation and rested in that thought.

On Friday, June 7, I woke up to a beautiful day of sunshine. I dressed, had breakfast, and drove to my son's home. The day was lovely. That afternoon I drove back to Jacksonville for my one-year check-up for my hip replacement. I checked in at the registration desk on the first floor of the Davis Building and contacted a friend of thirty years who worked on the grounds to see if she could meet me on her break.

After X-rays of my hip had been taken, my friend met me at my next appointment in the surgeon's waiting room on the second floor.

I told her about the miracle of beautiful weather and the vision of the Lord standing in the boat, speaking to the winds and waves, saying, "Peace, be still." She was so excited when she heard me say that! Then she told me about a book she was reading. One of the sections in the book that impressed her so much was where the Lord commanded the elements to be still. What a blessing to have shared this special moment! She and I only visited about fifteen minutes since she had to get back to work. We hugged and said goodbye. I checked in with the receptionist at the desk and shared my testimony concerning my prayer for the storm to be sent out to sea.

She smiled and said, "It did go out to sea!"

Then she showed me her bracelet with the word "Mercy" on it. This was her way of witnessing when people would notice the word and ask her what it meant. My Mayo friend and I had "church" as we praised the Lord together. The receptionist and I continued the sharing. A few minutes later, I was called back to see the surgeon and an intern who read my X-rays and had me walk back and forth so they could see how I was adjusting to the artificial hip. I received a good report and was dismissed.

Later in the evening, I was asked by a friend to have supper with her along with her daughter, and granddaughter and shared the testimony with them concerning the storm going out to sea. We all were blessed by sharing examples of God's faithfulness to us. Saturday, June 8, I drove back to Marianna in beautiful weather. I was a bit tired from my six hundred mile-round of driving, but full of joy and thankfulness because of the love and watch-care of the Father as He directed my path and gave me another perfect trip.

Ask Yourself...

As I read this section, what events in my life reminded me of God's protection over me and my family?

Record these events in your journal and be prepared to share with others His love and protection.

Read Proverbs 3:6.

What is God's promise to you concerning His protection over you?

How has this section changed the way you pray for your travel and the safety of your family members?

PART TWELVE
TESTIMONIES OF
HEALING MIRACLES

-91-

BETTY'S HEALING

Betty, who was a member of our church in Pompano Beach, FL, had been suffering with cancer and for years. Many people had prayed for her healing. One day David, our friends Hollis and Clarinda, and I being led of the Lord, went to Betty's home and prayed with her family for her healing. The next week, she went to her Jewish doctor for her monthly checkup and blood test. He found no cancer cells! He re-checked the test and the result was the same as the first. He could not explain it.

She said, "I've been telling you God was going to heal me."

We rejoiced with her! Some of the church members did not rejoice in the healing and questioned why she was healed after our prayer. It reminded me of the reaction of the Pharisees and Sadducees to healing in the Bible. There was no rejoicing in the blessing of healing to the restored person. A critical spirit ruled. What was in their hearts came out. The selfish church members became "man-centered" in regard to the miracle, thinking the ones who prayed for healing were seeking glory instead of praising God for Betty's healing by God's mercy and grace. The healing was wonderful and no one could take away Betty's gift! She praised God for her miracle and our faithfulness to pray.

-92-

GOD'S DIAGNOSIS REVEALED

My mother called me with a prayer request one afternoon when we were living in South Florida. She told me that her brother, Preston, was in the hospital and had been diagnosed with cancer. I agreed I would pray for him and put his name on our prayer list at our church. As I began praying for Uncle Preston, the Lord spoke to me in my spirit and told me he did not have cancer. I also had a vision that Mother should call Corbin Butler and have him visit her brother, Preston. Corbin was a well-known pastor in the Savannah area, a childhood friend of Preston and our family. He was known as a man of power in prayer who went to all the hospitals and prayed for every patient he could pray for, as well as many others who needed prayer in his community.

Preston had been concerned for years about the fact he had killed enemy soldiers in World War II, fearful that he would go to Hell for his actions. He suffered with Post Traumatic Syndrome Disorder, waking up many nights, screaming from dreams as he relived the horrors he went through as a medic in the Army. The experiences of war led to him to become an alcoholic. God gave me the knowledge that if Corbin could spend time with Preston and pray with him, then Preston would find assurance that God would forgive him for these acts in time of war and grant him peace.

I asked Mother to contact Corbin. He visited Preston in the hospital several times, toward the end of his life, giving godly counsel. Preston found peace with God during those times. Preston's doctor told the family that further testing showed he had no cancer, just as the Lord had told me through His Spirit. The accurate diagnosis was Pancreatitis, a condition that the doctor said was probably a result of years of alcohol consumption. Family members who sat with Preston in the hospital room the last few weeks of his life said he was speaking softly and as they leaned toward him to hear his words, they realized he was quoting the Twenty-Third Psalm. Day after day he would repeat the Psalm.

He seemed confident the Lord was His shepherd and he rested in that confidence.

Witness to the Indian

One Sunday morning, a lady in my Sunday School class asked the class members to pray for an American Indian she had met at the local hospital who did not know the Lord as his savior. She said he was dying and needed special prayer. I had an appointment at the hospital for a scheduled mammogram the next day, so I decided to go by and meet the man, if possible. When I got to the room, the man was conscious, but as I spoke to him I realized he might not be able to communicate very well.

A nurse came in to get him ready for transfer to a hospital in Dothan, Alabama where he could get special treatment. I told her I would step out of the room if she preferred, but she told me I could stay. When I prayed on Sunday as to how the Lord wanted me to witness to him, I felt He was leading me to sing a hymn. I had brought my old Broadman hymnal with me and sensed the Lord wanting me to sing a great hymn I felt would witness to the Native American. I told him why I was there and that I wanted to sing the message in the hymn for him if that was all right. He said I could. The words seemed so appropriate. I sang the great hymn, "My Faith Has Found a Resting Place" as the nurse went out of the room and later returned. I prayed the words below, written by Ms. Lidie H. Edmunds in the 19th century, would reach into the heart of the dying man.

"My faith has found a resting place, not in device or creed;
I trust the Ever-living One; His wounds for me doth plead,
Enough for me that Jesus saves, this ends my fear and doubt;

A sinful soul, I come to Him, He'll never cast me out.
My heart is leaning on the Word, the written Word of God,
Salvation by my Savior's name, salvation through His blood.
My great Physician heals the sick, the lost He came to save;
For me His precious blood He shed, for me His life He gave."
(Refrain)
"I need no other argument, I need no other plea;
It is enough that Jesus died, and that He died for me."

I continued to sing all the verses although he appeared to sleep or tune me out. When I finished the hymn, I told him what the scripture said about sin and the Savior. He told me that his grandmother had raised him to follow the "Indian way" and that was what he believed. A few minutes later, he was placed on a stretcher and taken out of the room to the ambulance that would move him to a hospital in Dothan. I knew I would never see him again.

A few days later, I saw the lady who had asked for the Sunday School class members to pray for the man. I asked her if she knew how he was. She told me he died the day he was taken to the Dothan hospital. What a dreadful feeling I experienced when I heard those words. I had no assurance that he was with the Lord, but I knew I would be blessed because I was faithful to witness to him. Had I not been scheduled for the appointment at the hospital the day he was taken to Dothan, and not acted on God's prompting to witness, I would have missed that chance to share the Good News of the Gospel with him.

It drives home the fact we must be ready at all times to give "the reason for the hope that lies in us" as the scriptures admonish us.

KNEE PROBLEMS

After about ten years of hard work and standing most of the time, I was aware of a great deal of pain in the left knee. The knee had been damaged from a fall when I was tripped by a blind friend's cane as she walked beside me years before. I prayed for a shot of some kind to be discovered that would replace the fluid in the knee, keeping the bones from rubbing against each other and reduce the pain. A year later, a friend who went to my church and knew about my specific prayer told me there was no such shot. This news did not discourage my exercise of faith. I continued to pray for the injection to become available.

Another year passed and someone told me there was a type of shot being considered, but it had not been approved by the Food and Drug Administration. I prayed all the next year for God to meet this need in His time. The same friend told me after a church service one day that the shot I had prayed for these three years had been approved by the FDA, but few doctors were trained in giving the shots. Someone else in the group of friends nearby heard the conversation and told me there was a doctor in Marianna who could give the injections. That amazed my friends, but I was not surprised.

The Lord always answers prayers in His time, in His way, and gives me every good and perfect gift.

In July of 1998, I began a series of Hylagen shots in my left knee once a week for five weeks. The doctor also gave me the injections in the right knee as a possible preventative for arthritis that might occur. Another series of shots could be given after six months to a year depending on the pain level and my need for relief. I did not return for additional shots until April of 2000, for another five weeks of injections. The Lord tells us we have not because we ask not according to James 4:2-3.

We can come boldly before the throne and ask
anything in His will, in His name,
and He will do it. I have found it so!

His Dark Cloud

As I lay down on my bed one night, something caused me to look up and over to the left side of the ceiling. There was a small dark cloud-shaped presence that fascinated me as it hovered above me. I knew in my heart it was the Lord. I reached up to touch it, yet knowing I could not. The Lord spoke to my spirit through His Spirit and said, "You are being healed." I did not know if that meant physically since I had problems with my knee or if it meant spiritually, emotionally, or financially. I only knew it was the Lord.

I said, "Lord, I'm not sure what that means, but I'm just glad you are here!"

I kept watching the cloud as it hovered over that spot until it faded away. Then I just lay there, dwelling in the moment, and thanked the Lord for visiting me in such a special way.

The next day at church, I realized the Lord wanted me to share the message with others. I told four individuals I saw on the way into the sanctuary what God had said and how He came to me in the night. They were receptive to the message. Later, when I was on the platform singing with the Praise Team, I asked the Minister of Music if there was a place in the service I could give a testimony. He told me it was a good time to go ahead and take the mike while I was in front of the congregation. I told the people present what had happened in my bedroom as the Lord came down in a special cloud to give me a message and that He had impressed me that I needed to share His words with someone who was present that day.

After the service, several of the people came up and asked me to tell them again what He said. I repeated, "You are being healed.

You are being healed," as I held each one in my arms. God is always in the healing business. It is a continual process, therefore the term "being healed."

**How good God is to come in His time and in His way
to those who will receive His message and share it
with others!**

GOD OF LIGHT

While reading through the Bible one morning, I began to wonder about the Lord appearing in the dark cloud. I knew that where He was there was light. I thought of the references I had read referring to God and light. As I pondered the visitation, I came across a verse in my daily reading from II Chronicles 6:1. The Lord said he dwelt in the dark cloud. Darkness and light are the same to Him. Wherever He is there is light. Just as I needed my experience cleared up and supported with scripture, He answered and increased my joy.

He is so faithful to me.

-97-

HEALING

A friend of mine who attended my church asked me to pray for her chronic foot problem. She was healed within the week. She had prayed over a period of time, but that week God answered with healing. All I did was be faithful to believe and pray as she asked. God sent her a miracle in His time.

Eating Disorder

Another church friend asked me on Wednesday night after choir practice, if I minded praying for his daughter who would not eat. She was about six years old and the family did not know how to help her nor why she refused food. The following Wednesday, I asked the father how she was doing. He said she had started eating a few days after he asked me to pray.

God, again, prompted the prayer and answered for His own good pleasure.

Ask Yourself…

The Lord tells us we have not because we ask not according to James 4:2-3.

Do I come boldly before the throne and ask in His will and in His name, believing He will do it?

Record in your journal when you begin to pray and ask God believing He will answer your prayer.

Read Psalm 103:3.

What is God's promise to you concerning healing?

How has this section changed the way you pray for yourself and for the healing for others?

PART THIRTEEN
MIRACLE HOUSE

-*99*-

MIRACLE HOUSE

In January 1996, I was singing a solo, "It Took a Miracle," in our Adult 7 Department at First Baptist Church in Marianna. After singing, I felt prompted to tell the group of older adults I was going to ask the Lord to give them all their miracles for 1996, speaking what I felt the Lord had impressed me to say. Then I realized the Lord spoke through me, to me, and that I would receive all my miracles, too. I told the group I was ready for the Lord to pour out all my blessings and had room to receive them, remembering the verse that says, "He will pour out such blessings that there will not be room to receive them." I opened my arms wide as I showed my willingness to receive.

The Lord began to show me miracle after miracle in the days to come. Some small, some large, but personal miracles for me to enjoy, praise Him for, and share with others. He sent me information through my spirit about our need for a house or some land for retirement. Somehow, I knew we would not build a house. I had always thought the Ed Woods house in Camellia Acres was so beautiful and was drawn to it from the first time I saw it in 1991 when it was the only house they had built on the 15 acres in which they had invested to develop as a subdivision. Soon after its completion, David had taken me by to see the house one day when we were riding around. It was one of the loveliest houses I had ever seen.

I said to him as we drove by, "Wouldn't you love to live in a house like that?"

He told me I could never live in a house like that house. We drove by and looked at it many times after that week. I was excited each time I saw it but never could have known what was in store for us. Mr. Woods began to build other houses to complete the Camellia Acres sub-division made up of about fourteen houses in phase one with plans to add twelve garden homes in what he named Camellia Gardens.

A friend of ours from First Baptist Church had some land she wanted to sell and asked for prayer in our Sunday School class the week after I told the Lord I was ready to receive all He had for me. The lady wanted us to pray she could sell the land in 5 or 10 acre lots. I told her we might be interested in a lot because the Lord had been dealing with me about "houses and lands." David and I went with her the next week to see the land she had for sale. It was undeveloped land, located about 20 miles from Marianna. Neither of us felt that the land nor the location was God's answer for us. Somehow, I felt our house would be nearer Blue Springs Baptist Assembly where we lived and worked.

The next step we took was driving by residential areas to look for houses. One of our friends from Chipola College who was a local realtor helped us look for a home within our price range. Our choices were limited by the amount we thought we could afford to pay. About this time, David's parents were having more serious health problems. In 1992, after we had taken turns going to their home to care for them a week at a time, they had moved to Marianna from Jacksonville, Florida, where they had lived over forty years. The Florida Baptist Convention had purchased a trailer park that was adjacent to the assembly. David was manager of the park and I posted the monthly rental checks.

His parent's moving to Marianna enabled us to help care for them, but within a few years, we realized we needed to take more responsibility for their care. They had moved into a single wide trailer with only one bathroom. Due to their health problems, this arrangement was not adequate for them. After about four years living in the trailer, they decided they wanted to look for a trailer with vinyl siding that had a second bathroom. They talked with David about the need to look for a double-wide trailer with more space around the same time the Lord had impressed me to consider "houses and lands."

David asked me one night after talking with them if I thought the Lord was asking us to consider finding a house suitable for a two-family dwelling to move his folks in with us. I realized the Lord was speaking to me about that, for what better reason to buy a house than to use it as a ministry to care for our elderly parents? This way it would not be a selfish venture but a way to please the Father and provide for the four of us. Things began to open up quickly at that point. His folks cried when we talked with them about our willingness to care for them and being interested in getting a house to live in together. They had cared for their elderly parents in their home years before as my mother and her brother had done for their mother also. The example was set before us and we were willing to take on the responsibility, knowing God would be pleased and blessings would be poured out on us as we "honored our father and mother" as He commanded in Exodus 20.

One day as I was reading in Jeremiah 32:6-12, I came across the verses that discussed buying a field. Later in the chapter, the Lord said, "Buy the field, for money and take witnesses." I was so excited. I called David to the room and read him the scripture. "What field?" he asked. I told him I did not know, but I was sure the Lord would tell me when the time was right. My joy was overflowing! We had seen one house a month before about the size we needed, in a location we liked, in a subdivision about three miles from the assembly. At the time, we did not think we could afford it but had kept it in mind and checked on its availability from time to time with our Realtor. In the meantime, the house sold. A friend from church heard we had considered buying the house and told us she was glad we did not buy it. She and her family had lived there when they first moved to Marianna. She said it was not well insulated and very hard to heat in the winter. What a blessing to have that confirmation that this was not the Lord's plan for us.

My next impression from the Lord was a vision of a large sign stating "home for sale by owner." I told David we would not be getting a house through our Realtor friend but would buy from an independent owner. He asked how we would go about finding a house "for sale by owner." I told him we would drive around and look where the Lord led us. While driving through Camellia Acres sub-division one day, David went by Ed's house, the dream house I had always said I thought I would love one like that if I could have "the desires of my heart."

God's promises are always faithful.

In Psalm 37:4, He says He will give the desires of their heart to those who delight themselves in Him. We could not imagine owning any house, much less Ed's mansion. Ed was a wealthy man and "licensed to sell houses in 48 states" as he told us when I first met him. He mentioned that he had taken a "little real estate course" years before and had done "quite well" as God had blessed him. He and Murl, his wife, were good stewards of what God had given them and had blessed many people through the years with the means God gave them.

As David drove by to look at the house that particular day, he saw a sign in the front yard which read "Luxurious 4/3 For Sale by Owner." Ed's phone number was listed on the sign as well as a Realtor's phone number, meaning Ed set up the listing so either he or the realtor could sell the house. David hurried back to the assembly where I was working in the office.

He was so excited as he asked me, "Would you like to go see your house?"

"My house?" I asked.

He said, "Yes, Ed Woods' house is for sale!"

We drove one mile to the house and began walking slowly around the house peeking in each window, trying to see as best we could. David was uncomfortable doing that after a short while. He said someone might see us and wonder why we were there. I felt the Spirit of the Lord strong within me as He let me know all I had to do was speak the words and they would come to pass.

My heart was pounding as I spoke the words He stirred up in my thoughts and I heard myself say, "No, someone will come out of one of those houses across the street and say they have a key and ask if we want to see the house!"

David stared at me as I turned around and looked across the street, knowing someone was going to do the very thing God had shown me would happen. It was amazing!

Peggy Parker opened her front door, as if right on cue, and said, "I have a key. Would you like to see the house?"

David kept staring at me and I kept beaming as I felt the power of the Spirit around me.

As Peggy came to the front door, I told her that I had wanted to see the house ever since it was built. It was arranged in such a way that David's folks could live on the right side with one bedroom used as a living room for them, as well as a bedroom for them with a private bath, and still, have an extra bedroom for guests with an adjacent bath. They would have their own hot water heater and air conditioning units separate from our side of the house, so we could all have the comfort level we preferred. Their shower had a place to sit on either end, as we had hoped we could have for their safety. The kitchen facilities and eating area could be shared by the four of us.

I had always wanted a little wallpaper if I ever had a house. The entire house was covered with pastel wallpaper of various patterns, except for one wall in the living room. On either side of the fireplace were built-in bookcases with storage cabinets above and below. If I could have designed the house, the built-in bookcases would have been one of the features I would have had added. My preference for window dressings was already in place also in the form of fabric covered vertical blinds, which matched the carpet. Blinds covered three sliding glass doors and one set of windows, overlooking a large deck with built-in seating available. The house was surrounded by trees and flowers.

When I looked out over the wooded area, I realized what the "field" reference meant in my Bible reading from Jeremiah. We were told the fifteen-acre subdivision had been a nursery covered in flowers and trees before the development started. The owners of the beautiful yellow house had planted all types of Camellias on the grounds and said something was blooming in the yard year-round. A "field" of flowers and trees, given to us by God, was a blessing, like having our own "garden of Eden." The only part of the house that was fully visible from the driveway going out to the street was the garage on the side of the house. The tree belt around us gave an abundance of privacy.

The large closets had my favorite type of shelving that I thought would be ideal if we ever had a house. Three rooms had recessed areas in the wall for TV sets which gave us more floor space. An alarm system was in place which automatically would call 911 in case of emergency. A double-car garage with automatic doors was ideal for the parent's car and for ours.

The Woods had moved to Macon, Georgia, about three weeks before we went through the house and decided to consider buying it.

There was a family member who had health problems and needed their assistance, so they moved to Georgia and built a home near the loved one. As things turned out, Ed was the one with failing health and died a few years later.

We talked to David's folks about the house and brought them by to see it. Then we contacted Mr. and Mrs. Woods by phone and discussed the price of the house as well as the terms necessary to purchase it. They drove down to visit with us and answer our questions about the house. The paperwork and the financing were taken care of by Ed and Murl who held the mortgage as they did with other properties they sold. Ed was a Christian businessman God had blessed greatly. Murl held Bible studies in their home in Marianna as well as in areas of Georgia where they had lived from time to time, as they would return to Georgia to take care of elderly family members. They had built four homes in Marianna, each time expecting to live there permanently to be near the area where Murl grew up, but they were not able to get the family members with special needs to move in with them, which necessitated their moving back to Georgia. Each of the Marianna homes was suitable for a two-family dwelling. God had us in mind when they built the two-family dwelling on Woods View Drive in Camellia Acres back in 1991.

Jesus tells us in John 14:3, "I go to prepare a place for you," and although He is referring to our heavenly home, I believe He has prepared each place for us to live while we are here on the earth.

As the scripture stated in Jeremiah 32, we "took witnesses" a few days after agreeing on terms for the purchase of the house, and signed papers in the pastor's office at First Baptist Church, Marianna. The Minister of Music and his wife, Mark and Lisa

Morris, were the Christian witnesses, as Christian owners sold the house to Christian buyers. I had sensed the night before that there would be a prayer at some point during the meeting. David called on Ed to pray before we signed the final papers. It was a lovely worship experience. A miracle of God had been given to us.

We discovered later that three families had been ready to buy the Woods home during the five months after they had moved to Macon. Each time something happened at the last minute to keep the house from selling. We knew in our hearts it was because God was saving it for us. We moved in April 1, 1996, and moved David's parents in on April 3. People in town began to hear about the sale.

As I was in town shopping on several occasions, people would come up to me, some I knew and some I did not know, and they would say, "I heard you bought the Ed Woods house?"

Each time I would answer, "Yes, it is a miracle of God." Many of them assumed we could not afford the house on our salaries working for a non-profit Christian organization. No one could deny the fact that God had worked a miracle in our lives. I felt for many years that it was not our house but His, given to us for a short while. How blessed to enjoy the house, perhaps until Jesus comes to get us and take us to another mansion He has prepared for us that is eternal in the heavens. He gave us yet another testimony to His greatness to those who serve Him and are "called according to His purpose" as He states in Romans 8:28.

We have claimed Romans 8:28 in our lives since our marriage and God has blessed us in spite of our frailties in the flesh.

-100-

ELDER CARE

We took care of both of David's parents for the first year after moving in the house. His daddy died a year later in our home at age eighty-four. The following year, we moved my mother in from Georgia. She had been diagnosed with Alzheimer's Disease and Dementia, but always knew what was going on and who we were. For several years, I called on Sunday afternoons each week to check with her care giver as to how Mother was and then would call my brother, Buddy and his wife, Rosa who lived in Savannah and see how they were doing. One Sunday morning, I felt strongly I should call immediately to check on Mother's condition. No one answered at her house. She could no longer use the phone, but one of the workers was always there with her. It was possible, I realized that she was in the hospital and I had not been informed by my family. I then called my sister-in-law and was told Mother had been in the Claxton Georgia Hospital for a few days with cystitis.

Rosa and Buddy had decided since they could not find anyone to care for her seven days a week, there was no other choice but to put her in a nursing home near her hometown in southern Georgia when she got out of the hospital. We had always agreed that we would take care of her and avoid a nursing home, if possible. Caretakers were paid during the week to care for her. My brother and I had taken turns covering Mother's weekend care as best we could, but we could find no one to work on the weekends when we could not be there. He lived thirty-five miles away from her home, but I lived 300 miles away which made it difficult for me to be with Mother more than one weekend a month.

Since Buddy and I were both on the way to our church services, he and I agreed to pray about the situation and talk after church. If they agreed, I planned to come get her. We talked after church and I reminded Buddy and Rosa that we did not need the nursing home for Mother because I was the optional choice. We had two Certified Nursing Assistants helping us already with David's mother and they were willing to help with my mother also. David and I drove six hours to Claxton, Georgia to get Mother from the hospital. When I arrived, Mother's doctor was getting ready to sign her into a nursing home. I told him I was the alternate solution. He said he was not aware of an alternate choice and she would have to be put in a nursing home eventually. I told the doctor we had Certified Nursing Assistants working for us at the assembly and they had also helped us care for David's folks and could help care for my mother also.

I asked Mother if she remembered the Mounties we used to watch on TV. She said she did. I told her I was like one of the Mounties who had come to rescue her. None of the friends or family in the hospital room seemed to be considering her preference and did not want her to know I planned to take her to Florida. They suggested I tell her I was going to take her home and make her believe she was going to her home. I could not do that out of respect to her. I told her the doctor was getting ready to sign her into the nursing home and asked if she would rather go there or home with me to Florida. She said she would rather go home with me, of course. The caregivers and family members in the room were amazed that I had been so open with her. I reminded them that she knew what was going on and needed to be considered in the decision. She just had trouble communicating her thoughts to us.

We had hoped Mother would get to live and die in her home, which was her preference, but that was no longer possible because she was so feeble and we had difficulty in getting caregivers to cover the weekends. She could no longer walk even with assistance and had to be moved about in a wheelchair.

After the paperwork was signed, I checked her out of the hospital. The friends and family standing by knew we had taken on a great task of caring for her in addition to caring for David's mother. We knew the Lord had given us a home that was prepared for us, so we could take care of the elderly and we had adequate help to do what was necessary. The willingness to care for our parents was put in our hearts by the Lord and we made ourselves available.

Mother was moved by an Emergency Medical Unit to Marianna that same day. It was a hard six-hour trip for her, but she did better than we thought she would. I road in the front seat with the driver and the other member of the medical team sat with Mother as she was secured on a bed in the back of the unit. David drove home and had arranged for a hospital bed to be set up before she and I arrived.

She lived only three months after coming to stay with us, dying at age eighty-six. We were so glad we had the opportunity to care for her in our home with the help of our two CNA friends who took turns staying, one at night and the other during the day, so we could cover our responsibilities at Blue Springs Baptist Assembly. Mother began to lose more of her communication skills. It was difficult for her to get her words formed and most of the conversation with her had to be answered by "yes" and "no."

She sat in her wheelchair one night at supper and watched me clear the table and start washing the dishes. She wanted to help but knew she could not. The expression on her face showed how sad she was.

She whispered, "I don't know how, don't know where, don't know when, don't know what."

I told her I did not know either, but we loved each other and David and I would take care of her as long as we could. She seemed to think that was okay but wanted to go back to her home in GA. I knew she was trying to say she wanted to die in her own home.

She had not spoken clearly for days but as we were watching Dr. Charles Stanley on TV preaching one Saturday night on being born again, she leaned over from her wheelchair and said slowly but clearly, "I'd rather, be saved, by grace."

That was so exciting to me! What a blessing! If she could only say one clear sentence, that was one I would have loved to hear! Mother died in September of 1998. She finally got to go back "home" for her funeral service and was buried in the cemetery lot beside my Daddy and other members of our family.

-101-

ALIVE FOREVER

The day Mother died, I called the Hospice nurse and the funeral home representatives. After the Hospice chaplain and other officials had visited with us and left the house, the body was removed and the hospital bed folded down by Michael who worked for a Health Equipment company and taken to the garage for pick up. It was a blessing that he and his family were visiting us that day and could help in this way. I was drawn to the bookshelf in the living room where Mother's 8 X 10 picture was placed. As I looked into her face, I could see life in her eyes as her spirit was nearby and in my spirit heard her say, "I'm alive!" I smiled and said, "I know!" It was a wonderful experience the Lord allowed us to have and a joyful moment.

**I knew she was alive forevermore,
but how dear of the Lord to allow us this special
spiritual connection.**

David's mother lived another five years, dying at age ninety-three. She was in a nursing home for seven months due to the fact David was diagnosed again with cancer and we did not know how much care he would need. The nursing home was about a mile from our home, so we were able to visit with her often. God took her mercifully in her sleep two months before her ninety-fourth birthday.

HOUSE PAID OFF

I prayed we would pay off the house in five years. We had already lived in the house about three years at the time. Through some amazing events, God helped us pay off our twenty-year note in eight years! David's folks helped pay part of the expenses; a CD from Mother's account was divided between Buddy and me, and that money was put on our house note; and when the interest rates changed, Mrs. Woods, who held the note gave us the better rate. She had allowed us to lower the monthly payments due to our expenses. There were no penalties for paying off the house early.

We give God the glory for the payoff.

Ask Yourself…

Do I focus on the positive things God is doing in my life or do I allow negative circumstances to control my thoughts?

Record the positive events in your journal every day and be sure to thank God for all His blessings. Ask Him how to use what appears to be negative for His glory as well.

Read Philippians 4:8.

What is God's instruction to you concerning how you are to focus your thoughts?

How has this section changed the way you think about both positive and negative circumstances in your life?

PART FOURTEEN
DAVID'S CANCER-MIRACLE
AFTER MIRACLE

-*103*-

CANCEROUS TUMOR

In December 2000, David noticed that he had an increasing lack of energy and seemed to become weaker and weaker. After retirement from the FL Baptist Convention Camps and Assemblies Department, months before, David was hired by the Jackson County School Board as an Interpreter for Deaf students. Often during that school year he would come home from work exhausted and had to go to bed. I encouraged him to see his doctor and have a checkup. He put it off several months, then realized he had to find out why he had no energy. The doctor put him in the local hospital for tests and found that had been losing blood over a period of time. His blood count was six. The doctor ordered three units of blood to be administered. After the transfusion, David felt much stronger. The large tumor that showed up on the X-rays on the outside of the colon had been the cause of the blood loss. The doctor told David it was necessary for him to see a surgeon at that point.

The surgeon in Dothan, Alabama, scheduled surgery for the last week in January 2002, to remove the rare Gastro Intestinal Stromal Tumor referred to by the acronym, GIST, a terminal condition. The day of the surgery, we drove over to the hospital in complete peace, resting in the Lord and enjoying the snow flurries, a rare sight in Alabama and Florida. David was taken to the OR as scheduled and some family members and I visited and prayed that all would go well. A few hours later, the surgeon came out to tell us the surgery was successful. He said the tumor was in a good place for him to remove it easily. As a precaution, he removed six inches of intestine. He told us the tumor had been growing slowly for years undetected. He did not know whether it was cancerous or not but said we would be notified in about a week. A week later when we had not heard back from the lab, we called to check on the status of the tumor and were told on a scale of 1 to 9, it was a 9 by cell count, a cancerous tumor. The doctor told us there was no need for further treatment. However in his opinion, if the cancer "came back" there was a 90 percent chance that it would be in the liver.

We thanked God for His care and concern.
We continued to testify to God's faithfulness to us.

David went back to work in the school system interpreting for the Deaf students as he regained his strength. Seven months later, he had to have surgery to repair a hernia. The surgeon also removed David's gall bladder when he found it was diseased. His recovery from this surgery seemed more difficult for him than the removal of the tumor in January. Two surgeries this close together were quite an ordeal for him. He had never been in the hospital for any reason prior to the cancer surgery except to have his tonsils out at age four. He was amazed how "involved the procedures were" as he put it. I told him that was why so many people wanted to tell about their operations if they could find anyone who was interested in listening. He seemed surprised he was so willing to share the details of the ordeal with friends and family who came to see him while he was in the hospital and when was recuperating at home.

-104-

LIVER CANCER

We were still caring for David's mother in our home about a year later when he and I began exercising at a fitness center near our home. He lifted weights each day while I worked out in the pool. We took turns going to the facility and staying with his mother. He ate very little and worked hard to lose weight. In a short while, he had lost forty pounds. I began to notice he looked jaundiced and he had dark circles under his eyes.

One day I told him, "Your cancer is back. You need to see your doctor."

He said there was no way I could know that, but I was sure the Lord let me know so I could warn him. He did not look well. He delayed going to the doctor for about a month. When the doctor examined him and ran tests, it appeared that David had lesions covering the liver. His doctor scheduled a PET scan to be taken two weeks later to make sure of the diagnosis. The scan was inconclusive due to "shadows" in the liver that we were told could be gas.

A further CT scan was done at the hospital a week later and the diagnosis of cancerous lesions in the liver was confirmed. The doctor was troubled and sorry to have to give him bad news. He told us to see an Oncologist as soon as possible. We told the doctor that we were in the hands of the Lord and were at peace.

Again, the Lord gave us an opportunity to testify according to the faith He had given us.

David decided to see an Oncologist in Dothan, Alabama, Dr. Brown, who had been his daddy's doctor a few years before. After looking over the reports from the Marianna doctor, the Oncologist discussed the seriousness of the diagnosis with us. Dr. Brown recommended an oral chemotherapy pill called Gleevec made by Novartis Pharmaceutical Company. It had been approved by the Food and Drug Administration just a year before David needed it. We were told the pill had fewer side effects than intravenous chemotherapy and was more convenient to take. It was designed for the treatment of GIST tumors to slow down their growth. The doctor also asked if we would like to seek a second opinion and encouraged us to do so.

We had done some research on types of treatment and facilities that offered special programs for cancer patients. We discussed three options that David and I had considered. I had written to Cancer Treatment Centers of America and we had looked at a video their office had sent. We also read materials in the packet sent to us. We realized that was an excellent place to go for treatment, but would not consider flying to Texas and back on a regular basis.

When the doctor asked what we preferred doing, we told him we would like to go to Mayo Clinic in Jacksonville. There were several reasons for that choice: the reputation of Mayo for research, diagnosis, and treatment of disease, and the fact David had grown up in Jacksonville and knew the city well. Also, we had lived in the city for several years in the past and had many friends there and our daughter and family lived in the city. Our son and family lived in a town about an hour away, so it would be convenient for us to stay with either family overnight when David had appointments at the clinic.

When we had our first meeting with the Oncologist at Mayo Clinic, he asked if we had seen the CT Scan showing the condition of the liver. We had not, so he brought it up on his computer screen. Our son was with us that day, so the three of us looked at the pictures with the doctor. No one said anything. I suppose a picture was worth 1,000 words, as the saying goes. We stood there in silence.

Finally, I said, "What you are trying to tell us is that you will maintain life as long as possible and help David deal with pain."

The doctor seemed amazed at my concise statement and said, "Well, yes."

Then he told us he would suggest using a chemotherapy pill that had been accepted by the Food and Drug Administration about a year before called Gleevec. This confirmed what the doctor in Dothan had told us and we felt this was the best choice for treatment. David began the oral chemo treatment in September of 2003, taking 400 mg per day, two pills in the morning and two at night. He took prescribed pain pills as needed and additional supplements.

The first week of taking the medicine was difficult for him. He was sick to his stomach and very weak, staying in bed most of the time. I asked the Lord how I should pray for David and He showed me a vision of people in our living room, praying for him. I realized God wanted us to have a healing service. When I asked David how he felt about that, he agreed that we could ask a few people to come and pray. One of our friends in the church also needed special prayer for healing from Hepatitis C, so we invited she and her husband. Our pastor, music minister, their wives, our deacon, and eight other friends came to pray with us the following Monday night. David got out of bed and dressed for the service. I gave a testimony of the peace we had from the Lord to face the cancer.

The husband of the lady who was sick told the group what he, his wife, and four sons had gone through when they were told of her illness and how they were dealing with the trial. David and the lady, each gave testimonies, through their tears, but were confident that God was going to heal them. I asked our deacon to read from James 5:13-20 where the passage mentions calling on the leaders of the church to anoint with oil and pray for the sick to be healed. We gathered around David and our sick friend and prayed for the Father to heal them if that was His perfect will.

About a week later, David was feeling better and no longer needing to stay in bed. His jaundice was gone and he began to adjust to the medicines. He had some good days and bad days after that night of prayer, but was able to work full-time in the school system at Malone, FL as an interpreter for the Deaf, fill in as a substitute organist for two churches in Marianna, and lead music when our Minister of Music had to be away from his leadership position.

God continued to be merciful and give us numerous opportunities to witness for Him through his illness.

It seems people will listen to what you have to say if it concerns a physical problem that cannot be explained apart from a miracle of God. If He chose to take David at any time, we were ready to accept His will. If He chose to heal him completely, we would accept that miracle as well. Whether we live or die we are with the Lord and we praise Him for each day He gives us to serve Him.

**There is no "downside" for us as Christians!
We are blessed in the name of the Lord!**

-105-

MOUNTAIN HOUSE

We stayed in a cottage on top of a mountain in Mountain City, GA, near Clayton, owned by a Marianna neighbor in July 2005. The view from the deck was amazing. From that location we could see two or three little towns in the valley and several chains of mountains all around. The owners told us they bought on that spot for the view, not for the house. David was so excited about being there he wanted to buy a home in the mountains. He felt so much better up there that we even did some mountain climbing. I had a knee replacement just four months prior to the week of vacation. David had liver cancer, yet the Lord gave us the energy to climb two mountains that week!

Every day we drove around and looked at houses in the area. A friend of ours told us about a house for sale by a retired missionary couple. We made an appointment to meet with them and see their house. They lived in the Winter Park area of Florida six months out of the year and in the mountains the other half of the year. The wife wanted to sell the house and move into the home place where she grew up. We liked the house but did not feel that was where God was leading us. It was difficult to locate from the highway and was on a clay road. We preferred a house near a paved road.

In October of 2005, we had another week of vacation during Spring Break from David's school job. The little cottage with the great view was being used by the owners that week so we stayed at a Time Share exchange in Sky Valley, just inside the Georgia line and about a two-hour drive from Clayton. The winding road to the resort took us in and out of Georgia and North Carolina, right along the state lines. The scenery was beautiful although leaves had not changed to any great extent, due to a warmer dry season. Again, David wanted to look at houses to consider as a mountain house for our family to enjoy. We did a lot of driving each day.

One day, we were passing by a realtor's office on Highway 129 south of Blairsville, Georgia. David asked me if I thought we should stop and see what houses might be available for purchase.

I said, "Yes, I think so."

We went in and talked with the receptionist and after a short wait met the Realtor. She was very busy and had some appointments scheduled to show houses to other clients, but said she had a few minutes she could devote to our search within the price range we suggested. She printed out some sheets of information on the houses the computer selected and we began our search. Choestoe Village was a few miles from her business. We told her we had found that area and would love to see if anything was for sale on the creek side of the subdivision. The charming little village had about fifteen homes on the creek side and that many or more on the woods side. We had stopped one day while in that area and talked with a resident who was out in his yard. He told us that one lady on the creek side might be interested in selling, but her children did not want her to sell the house. We could see why. The Realtor showed us a two story, two-bed room, two-bath house with two extra lots, on the woods side of the acreage. It cost more than we had expected and the rooms were smaller than we preferred.

We had given the realtor our testimonies of God's saving grace and how He led us each day in miraculous ways. She was amazed and excited about the experiences we shared with her. She said she had heard Charles Stanley mention miracles happening like these to Christians who followed the Lord. We agreed that God performs miracles for all of us every day. She made an appointment to meet us at her place of business the next day to see more houses. In addition to the sheets of information she had given us, she printed out a few more for us to look at, on our own, for the rest of the day thought we could only view them from the outside. We listed them in order of preference. After seeing all the houses she suggested, we realized we were going to have to consider more expensive houses.

The next day we asked her to check on houses in a slightly higher price range. She entered information in the computer to see what might be available in that range and only one sheet came up from the printer.

The realtor looked at the sheet and then said, "Having known you people like I have the past two days, I think God must have saved this house for you. Look at the top right corner. The house is listed as 'expired' which means the contract on the house has expired and no one has been showing it for a long time. The price has been reduced also."

We read over the sheet of information and realized it was a good possibility for us to consider. The realtor drove us to the house so we could check it out. We were so pleased that is was on a paved road and had a paved driveway with a slightly steep grade up a knoll. Some of the other houses we had seen did not have good roads and had limited space in the driveway in which to turn the car around.

The two-story house had been completely remodeled inside and the basement had been closed in making it into a three-bedroom, three-bath house with a wood burning fireplace upstairs in the living room and gas logs in the downstairs den. When we saw the living room, dining room, kitchen combination with walls painted yellow, it was like walking into sunshine. Some of the rooms had colors that were too bright for us, having been chosen by the owner's daughter who was an artist. We knew after being there a short period of time, we had found our mountain home!

The preliminary paperwork was ready for us to sign at the realtor's office the next day.

We returned to Florida and began checking with several banks before deciding where to get our loan. After contacting six financial institutions, we settled with a Marianna bank. The loan went through in less than two weeks! The sellers had a deadline to meet in order to purchase their house in New York where they were moving to take care of the husband's mother, so time was at a premium for the closing.

**God worked out all the details and
led us through open doors, literally.**

A young builder had asked us a few months before if he could buy one of our lots in Indian Springs. At that time, we were not interested in selling, but now we wanted to use the money to pay off a portion of the loan. We contacted him to see if he still wanted the lot. He was interested and in three weeks he bought the second lot. The young couple who bought our first lot told us about someone they knew who wanted to buy some land and build a house, so we contact her. She met us a week later and gave us a binder on the lot. She had some problems working out her loan with her bank, but in a month's time the three of us met to sign papers and we had a check for the third lot. In our first two payments on our loan, we had paid 45 percent of the purchase price. We had made a profit on the lots that far exceeded our expectations.

**God continues to bless us beyond measure and
use us for His glory.**

-106-

INSURANCE DILEMMA

After my husband's sixty-fifth birthday, our group insurance coverage changed from Blue Cross Blue Shield to Medicare as our primary insurance and Hartford Insurance as our secondary coverage with our company plan. Prior to this birthday, BCBS had covered his monthly liver cancer medicine which cost $2650. Our co-pay was only $15.00 the first year the medicine was prescribed by his doctor at Mayo Clinic in Jacksonville, Florida. The second year our co-pay went up to $25.00. We were so thankful for the good coverage. The medicine cost went up to $4000 for the monthly bottle of pills in 2006, and David was told his cap for payment on prescription drugs for the year was $5000. He would use that up in six weeks.

When David turned in his request in March for the controlled substance, he was told our co-pay would be around $3000. Taking the prescribed 600 mg of Gleevec per day, our cost would be $600 each day. We could not pay that amount. We were also told that our cap for prescriptions for the year was $5000 per person. When the $5000 was reached, we would be expected to pay full price for our prescriptions. After praying about the situation, we contacted our friend, the insurance representative for the Florida Baptist Convention, to see what he would suggest. In addition to contacting him, we looked into other insurance prescription plans with various companies who did not require a physical exam due to David's condition.

A friend at Mayo Clinic in Jacksonville, who works in billing and insurance, suggested we contact Novartis, the manufacturer of

Gleevec and see what they could do for us. Two of the insurance companies we contacted and the Oncologist's nurse in Dothan also suggested we contact the manufacturer and make an appeal for assistance, turning in the necessary paperwork they required. She told us normally those patients who had insurance and assets would be turned down. If this happened, she said we were to appeal again, and that the process would take several weeks. We did not have that much time to get David the medication he needed. David, the insurance representative for the Convention, and a representative of the drug manufacturer, Novartis, set up a three-way call to discuss the matter a week after we were told about the cost.

By that time, David had been without his cancer medicine for a week. It was necessary for him to take an additional pain pill daily to help with his discomfort. The criteria for helping us depended on our income, assets, and whether we were covered by insurance. David answered all the questions and the Novartis representative filled out the necessary papers as they talked. The representative said it looked as though we would be denied assistance for the cost of the drugs. Our only hope was that the Lord would miraculously work things out according to His will.

Remembering that I had encouraged him to have our estate put in a Living Trust in April of 2004 and that we had set that up with the Convention lawyer's help, David asked the Novartis representative if the Living Trust would make a difference in our getting assistance. He said if we had a Living Trust, he could send the medication out to us the same day at little or no cost and we would have the medicine by 10 A.M. the next day! In a moment everything had changed! David was told that in a year's time he would be evaluated again to see if he still qualified for the assistance. The medicine was to be sent to us by UPS each month, on the day David needed to start the next twenty-eight-day supply.

God worked it out in one simple question about a Living Trust, something He prompted us to set up two years before it was needed.

**The Lord always prepares a way in advance,
even when we might not see it or realize all its benefits.**

David began to have terrible pain in his right shoulder the night of April 4. The pain radiated down his right side and into his stomach. I took him to the Emergency Room at our local hospital. After an EKG, two X-rays, and a CT Scan, he was given several shots of morphine. The doctor on duty asked if we would like for him to give us some pain medicine for him to take at home. The morphine was helping very little at that point, so we ask that he be admitted. He continued to have pain into the next day and began to run low-grade fever. The doctor could not find the reason for the temperature. We assumed there was infection, possibly due to a blockage behind the left kidney that had shown up on the CT Scan.

The day the medicine was supposed to be delivered, David was still in the hospital. I stayed home to receive and sign for the medicine on Thursday of that week. When 12 P.M. came and the medicine still had not been delivered, I called Novartis and asked for the same representative who had helped us the day before. He was in a meeting and another representative took my call. The representative told me we had to sign up for Medicare Part D in order to get the medicine. I knew that was incorrect and told him we could not apply for Medicare Part D without losing our Hartford prescription plan, according to information we had received from our insurance representative from the Convention. The man on the phone insisted I fill out the papers for Part D that would be sent to us by fax. He also told me the medicine would take two days to arrive. I knew this was conflicting information from what we were given by our insurance representative with the Convention.

The Novartis representative had already worked out these details for us to receive the medication overnight.

I asked for the tracking number for the delivery so I could call UPS and find out when the drugs would arrive. The company representative was not prepared for that request. I was told to hold while he checked on the information. While I was waiting for him to return to the phone, I opened up my Word Document, "Miracle in My Life" and begin to type the latest miracle of the day, knowing the Lord was working all things together for our good. As I was typing in the computer file, I heard the doorbell ring.

I said aloud, "Jesus, do you suppose that is David's medicine?"

I knew He had sent the medicine we needed! I laughed as I went to the door and opened it. There was the UPS delivery man standing on our porch with the chemo medicine! I told him about our adventure of the past two weeks and he rejoiced with me to see God's hand in it all. The delivery man was a Christian and remembered seeing us when he made deliveries at Blue Springs Baptist Assembly when we were employed there. He assured me he would see that our pills were delivered on time each month and if I had any questions about a delivery to call him.

David started the medication that day. He was in the hospital until the April 8 due to a fever and being so weak. The doctor released him after four days. He stayed in bed until the eleventh when we went to see his Oncologist for his monthly appointment in Dothan, AL. Dr. Brown realized when he saw the red blood count that David was losing blood. The count had dropped to 8.3 in one week. He was given a new medicine by injection, called Aranesp, to build up his blood. The drug had just been approved by the FDA the day before our appointment and was to be given in the 500 mg dosage.

**We could see God's hand working on our behalf,
just when we needed Him most.**

David was to receive another injection of Aranesp at his next appointment with Dr. Brown. Dr. Brown was cautious and preferred David be given the shot instead of a blood transfusion which carried some risk. If the two shots did not bring the blood count up, a transfusion would have been the next obvious choice.

The Mayo Clinic appointment to see Dr. Kim had been set up for April 21. We called to see if the doctor felt it necessary to see him sooner due to the problems he was having the days he had been off the medication. The doctor told us to keep the same appointment and give the medication time to work in his system. The miracle of the medication was that it was designed to bring the body back to its previous state in case the patient missed dosages for some reason. How amazing!

When David went to Mayo Clinic in Jacksonville for the April appointment, he had the usual blood work, CT Scan, and consultation with his doctor. As we looked over the CT Scan with the doctor, he told us the cancer had eaten through some of the liver tissues and caused the liver to bleed. That was the reason for the blood loss. He agreed with the treatment Dr. Brown had prescribed but said if the blood count did not come up to a proper level in the next few weeks, that he would recommend a blood transfusion.

We asked about the blockage near the left kidney. Dr. Kim told us it was a cyst and had shown up on the CT Scan before. Since the liver situation was more serious, the cyst had not been addressed. We were told that David should stay on the same medicine since we had a hard time getting approval for coverage. The doctor had planned to put David on another cancer pill that had been developed, but he said it was more expensive than the Gleevec David was presently taking. He was very concerned about the cost of the drugs and the fact so many people are unable to be treated with medicine that would actually help their health conditions.

God continued to work in David's body and give him strength to return to work, interpreting for the deaf children at the local school.

-107-

NEW DRUGS

On August 3, 2006, David had an appointment for tests at Mayo Clinic. He was told the CT Scan showed the tumors in his liver had doubled in size since the April appointment. After three years on the Gleevec chemo pills, they were no longer helping his incurable condition. In July 2006, Novartis Pharmaceuticals had approved his assistance on the drug cost for Gleevec until the end of the year, but now Dr. Kim wanted David to try a new drug approved by the FDA called Sutent, manufactured by Pfizer Pharmaceutical. This meant the process for assistance had to be started once more. This time we had all the necessary papers in a file and only had to make copies to send to Pfizer. When we got home, I looked up the information on the internet for Pfizer assistance programs, contacted the toll-free number, and requested an application for patient assistance to be faxed to us as soon as possible. When the form arrived, David filled out all the necessary sections for the patient and we mailed the form to Dr. Kim at Mayo for his section of the form to be filled in with his signature, stating the patient had to have this particular drug. The request was sent by Priority Mail and I asked that Dr. Kim have the form sent back by Priority or quickest mailing available.

A week went by and I called to see why we had not received the form, wondering if Dr. Kim had mailed it to Pfizer or not signed it yet. In the meantime, David continued taking the prescribed amount of Gleevec chemo pills he had on hand and continued his supplements. The nurse I spoke to was concerned about the situation and called me back after checking on the problem. The

Priority envelope was located, Dr. Kim signed the physician's form and mailed it to us. When his information arrived at our home the end of August, we sent it with the other fifteen pages of personal information to Pfizer Connection to Care with a request for a signed card stating when the packet was received.

After not receiving the signed card for over a week, I called to check on the status of the packet. They told me that the request had been received, assistance was denied, and the packet was being sent back to us. The representative suggested we try another one of the nine Pfizer assistance plans, starting with the First Response program. The representative said it would take us about two weeks for the request to be processed. That same day, I called Mayo Clinic in Jacksonville to let them know the situation and the fact we needed their help in contacting First Response. The nurse on duty looked up the information on the internet and printed out the necessary forms. Dr. Kim signed the request for assistance. We faxed our recently filed income tax form along with our original request for assistance to Mayo Clinic. The nurse then sent in all these forms to First Response Assistance Program for their consideration.

On September 12, I received a call from a representative from Pfizer First Response to inform us that since we had no "pharmacy assistance coverage," David had been approved to receive Sutent "free" for six months. It was to be delivered to our home by McKesson Delivery Service within 24 hours after McKesson Specialty Pharmacy received a signed prescription from Dr. George Kim at Mayo. They were to send the fax to him on September 12 and he was to return it that day.

**The miracle we had requested had been granted by
our all-powerful God!**

After giving my testimony about the trust we had in the Lord and all the prayers of friends and family in various parts of the world, I discovered Scott, our Pfizer First Response representative, was a Christian. We had a great time sharing our faith, acknowledging the miracle God had granted, and enjoying the fellowship we felt for each other as His children.

In six months, we were evaluated again to see if we qualified for coverage of the meds and again sent in the necessary paperwork. In a few weeks, we got a call saying Pfizer First Response would cover David's Sutent for another six months. God continued to answer the prayers of His people and provided the chemo medication Dr. Kim prescribed.

-108-

AUSTRALIA/MALAYSIA MUSIC MISSIONS TRIP

David started taking the Sutent pills on September 15, 2006, just five days before we left on the overseas music mission trip with 188 of the Florida Baptist Singing Men and Women and family members. The trip was for fourteen days and David was concerned about his adjustment to the pills and any possible side effects. We traveled approximately 50,000 miles from Jacksonville, FL, to Atlanta, GA, to Los Angeles, to Taipei, Taiwan, to Kuala Lumpur, Malaysia, to Sydney, Australia, back to the United States and home to Florida. Our group sang in a total of nineteen churches. David and I sang in nine concerts, including one at the Salvation Army and a concert at the Sydney Opera House while in Australia where the Gospel was presented in song and through the pastor who traveled with our group. Officials at the Sydney Opera House gave our group the new name Florida Worship Choir to fit on their marquee.

The trip was wonderful and inspiring as we shared the message we were sent to give to the people of the nations. David was very tired but did get some rest on the flights. He did not have any noticeable side effects from the new medicine except the first day of the trip at Los Angeles airport before the overseas flight. God answered our prayers by His grace. He consistently gave us the desires of our hearts and allowed David to keep up the pace of the trip taking part in the activities although he was weak. Our group was kept safe during all our travels and we were blessed to be used of the Lord.

We were reminded of the scriptures that tells us in our weakness the Lord is seen to be strong.[1]

---

[1] 2 Corinthians 12:10

-109-

THE OVER-NIGHT MIRACLE

After one year, the coverage through Pfizer Pharmaceutical Company was discontinued. We received a call from one of the representatives and were told the October shipment was the last one we would receive from Pfizer. I contacted Patient Services, Inc. to ask for their assistance. The necessary paperwork was faxed to PSI as soon as I could get the information updated and compiled. About once a week, I would call to check on the progress of the petition. The decision was made not to cover the expense for the drug due to our combined yearly income being over the allowed amount. The representative gave me some guidelines I could use to show the need for financial assistance in getting the drugs. I faxed our second request for paperwork.

After a few weeks, additional paperwork was required including an updated Social Security letter stating current income. David was due to start the medication on November 8. I told Wanda, the PSI representative for David's case, we would be in Dothan on the seventh for him to have hand surgery. In faith, I asked the representative to call our cell phone with the news that we would be covered for the cost of the meds. After the surgery on November 4, I received a call on my cell phone from Wanda saying the McKesson Specialty Pharmacy had requested one more letter from Social Security to be faxed to PSI. The Social Security office was nearby, so we drove there and requested that the letter be faxed immediately. When the letter was received, Wanda called from PSI and told me she was faxing the letter on to MSP.

When we arrived home from Dothan about 6 p.m., we received a call from McKesson requesting a credit card number so the meds could be sent. I asked the meds be shipped "overnight" in order for David to start back on the pills and was assured that would be the case. The Sutent was delivered to our home the next morning, as scheduled.

Yet another miracle God worked out for us as
He rewarded the faith He gave.

-110-

SUTENT FAILS

The adventure continued as we went to Mayo Clinic in Jacksonville for David's next appointment on December 14, 2007. Dr. Kim looked over the CT Scan and told David the Sutent was "no longer working" for him. He said we had three basic choices: (1) David could choose to stay on the Sutent; (2) He could have Intravenous chemo which usually was not effective for GIST tumors; (3) He could consider clinical trials. There was little choice. When we returned home, I spent about three days looking up hospitals on the internet, trying to find a facility doing clinical trial for GIST. There was only one hospital near us conducting the trials for David's type of tumors and that was Moffitt Cancer Center in Tampa. I contacted Bonnie, a representative whose phone number was listed on the internet. A few days later, she returned the call saying we should "get Robert down here" right away.

An appointment was scheduled for Robert David McCormick on January 15, 2008, for testing to see if his general health was good enough to start the trials. Fellow members of the Baptist State singing group, The Florida Worship Choir, invited us to stay in their home in Tampa. We drove down on the January 14 and went to the Clinical Research Unit for the appointment the next day. After the blood draw, EKG, and urinalysis, we were free to drive back home. This was to be one of many 660 mile-round-trips we took to be a part of the clinical trials.

We returned on January 30 for further tests and were told that David did qualify for the trials which were to begin on February 11 for a fourteen-hour day, 7 A.M. to 9 P.M. On February 11,

259

we arrived at Moffitt Cancer Center at 7 A.M. David was given 800 mg of Vorinostat, a new chemo pill, to see if his heart could tolerate it. The dosage was too strong for him to stay on, but we were told the dose would be cut down to 400 mg in the next stage of the trial. There were blood draws and EKGs done every few hours by Vance, the nurse assigned to take care of David. We were staying with our friend Ron that night in Valrico, Florida. During one conversation with Vance about our lodging, we found out he had gone to Junior High School with Ron's daughter, who is now married to the director of our Florida Worship Choir. That was a surprise for Vance and for us.

The Vorinostat caused his white blood cells to drop significantly, so he was taken off the pills. This occurred three times during the fourteen weeks of trials. May 30, we were told the drug had failed to be effective in treating the lesions in David's liver. He was offered an opportunity to start another trial on two combined drugs. The trial was to start in a matter of weeks. We were given the booklet of information concerning the new trial medication. After reading the materials, we told the medical team we would consider being a part of the clinical trials and give them our answer in a week or so.

After we had prayed about the decision, we decided we should not begin the new trial. Dr. Thomas W. Brown had monitored David's blood work for five years and we decided we would ask him to take over David's case. It was more convenient to drive the 45 miles to Dothan than it was to continue treatment in Jacksonville or other cities several hours away. I requested David's records from Mayo Clinic and Moffitt Cancer Center to be sent to Dr. Brown's office in Dothan, so he would have access to all the information he needed. At David's appointment with Dr. Brown the first week in June, Dr. Brown prescribed Gleevec chemo pills for David, hoping his body would accept it as a "new" medication.

I contacted Patients Services, Inc. to request financial assistance for coverage of the medication. The 2008 price for the pills was $6840.00 for one month's supply. One of the representatives sent me the paperwork to fill out for the request. I filled out the forms and sent them back by fax. In a few weeks, I was contacted and told the medication for the month of June would be provided free of charge, with PSI paying McKesson Specialty Pharmacy the total amount due, as long as Caremark Prescription Drug plan was covering the prescription drugs.

Due to the limited coverage cap of $5,000 for David's prescription drugs for the year, I knew I would need to seek assistance through Novartis Pharmaceutical Company, maker of the drug for the next month's drug supply. I began the paperwork process after checking on what was required for the company's consideration of the matter. In July, PSI contacted me to let me know that the Caremark plan no longer was assisting in the cost of the drugs as the $5,000 cap had been used up in June. PSI offered to pay 50 percent of the cost for July with the remainder of about $3,000 being charged to us.

David contacted Jayme Alfano, the Mass Mutual insurance rep for the Florida Baptist Convention, and asked him to request the money for two months' charges to be taken from David's annuity with Mass Mutual. Jayme requested the check to be sent but told us it had to be sent to our home address. Due to the fact we were in North Georgia, we asked a neighbor in Marianna to send the envelope from Mass Mutual to the mountain house address as soon as it arrived. The check came in a few days, so I called McKesson Specialty Pharmacy to request them to ship the medicine by July 17. The medicine arrived on the eighteenth by Federal Express delivery.

I called Novartis to see what progress had been made on the petition for assistance, knowing the August medicines would also cost another $3,000 with PSI paying 50 percent of the cost. The

Novartis representative said our petition had been turned down. I asked that we start the appeal process and was asked to fill out more forms that would be sent to me. When I completed those forms, I faxed them to Novartis. When the August meds were due to be shipped, I checked once again to see if Novartis would help with the cost of the meds. The representative said the matter had not been decided and requested a copy of the first page of our most recent tax return and statement of income. I faxed the information the next day.

A representative from MSP called and requested a check for $3,000 for the August meds. Once the check was received from David's Mass Mutual annuity and deposited in our bank account, I wrote a check and mailed it to cover our co-pay. David and I were in Marianna for about a week and then went on vacation to Kissimmee, Florida. I called twice during that time to check on the appeal process through Novartis.

On August 22, I was told David would be covered "free" for one year starting September 15, 2008, with coverage ending on Sept. 19, 2009! This was truly a miracle of God and we praised His name for His watch care over us.

God continued to lead us and bless us with His favor!

-111-

CT SCAN

In October of 2008, Dr. Brown scheduled a CT scan of David's liver. The doctor said the findings were multiple lesions in the liver, too numerous to count. The scan showed the lesions were growing and there was no indication that the Gleevec chemo pills were slowing down the growth. David continued to work at school and play the organ at church on Sundays, but had little energy most of the time. On December 29, 2008, a letter was sent from Novartis Patient Assistance Program stating David had to re-apply for enrollment in the assistance program to get his Gleevec, although he had been told he would be covered for free Gleevec chemo pills until September of 2009.

The Novartis Pharmacy had attempted to reach us by phone during the Christmas holidays, but we were in North Georgia and our answering machine was not working at our residence. We did not get their message to set up a date for delivery of his medication in January 2009. When the December 29 letter arrived, I called Novartis and asked for Chris, who was familiar with our case, but he was not available, so I talked with Sherri about the enrollment requirements. Sherri checked the computer records and saw NPAP had agreed to cover David for the meds for a year. According to Chris, the application had to be filled out and sent in again to update David's records. She told me that Novartis would supply the January medication so David would not be without his chemo pills.

On January 12, David called me from his job at the school and asked me to get him an appointment with his doctor. He was in a lot of pain. Dr. Brown was not going to be in his office in Dothan until late afternoon that day due to making rounds at the hospital in the morning hours. So, I asked that our friend, the principal of the school, to drive David to the ER at Jackson Hospital. I met David at the hospital and after three and a half hours, he was seen by the doctor on duty. Tests were run to see if the doctor could determine the reason for the new pain. The EKG was normal. The blood work showed the hemoglobin was low, but the hospital personnel could not give David a Procrit injection. We were told that the injection would have to be given by his doctor in Dothan on his next appointment which was January 19.

David returned home and continued taking his pain meds and resting as much as he could. He did not return to school on Tuesday, but on Wednesday he felt some better so he went to work. By that afternoon, he realized he had gone back to work too soon so he stayed home Thursday and Friday to rest. This was the most time he had missed at work since he started interpreting for the Deaf. He was disappointed he could not reach his goal of being on the job every day.

On January 19, David had his appointment with Dr. Tom Brown at Flowers Hospital. The paperwork for the application to Novartis was delayed until we could get the doctor's signature on one of the forms. Dr. Brown told us the liver enzymes were normal, which indicated the Gleevec was beginning to help the liver regenerate itself. That was wonderful news! The count had not been normal since he was diagnosed with GIST in 2003!

Dr. Brown always made an effort to give us positive news and encouragement. We were so pleased he was a Christian and shared the confidence we had in the Lord. David had a new health issue to discuss with Dr. Brown, however. There appeared to be a new hernia or the possibility that the repaired hernia done in 2003 had broken loose. We knew there was the possibility of more tumors also. The doctor agreed that it was probably a new hernia after a brief exam. David reminded Dr. Brown about the pain that caused him to go the ER at Jackson Hospital on January 12. The ER doctor at Jackson Hospital could not determine the cause of his pain in his left side, stomach, arm, and shoulder even after taking X-rays and an EKG.

The ER doctor had suggested further scans be done to see if the pain was caused from Pleurisy or the beginning of Shingles, although he saw no evidence of either of these from the X-rays. He said more detailed tests were needed and suggested they be done in Dothan with an order from Dr. Brown. David was due to have a CT scan in February 2009, to check the liver, a procedure that was done every four months routinely. After the exam and consultation concerning the liver situation, Dr. Brown told his nurse to set up an appointment with the Urologist at Flowers Hospital, just a few floors below the area where Dr. Brown had his office.

God worked out the details and David had an appointment two hours later.

The Urologist said that there was blood and/or fluid accumulating in the lower abdominal area manifesting itself in the scrotum. It was filled with the fluid, turning the skin a reddish purple. No treatment was suggested nor any further appointments made to see about the problem. The doctor said the situation would take care of itself. The CT scan to be taken in February was necessary to discover the source of the bleeding.

David had been without his Gleevec pills since January 18. I contacted Novartis on Tuesday after faxing all the necessary paperwork earlier that morning. The medicine had not arrived on Wednesday, so I called Sherri again and she let me talk with the lady in the Pharmacy. The overnight delivery was set up and the meds finally arrived about 11:15 A.M. on Thursday. It was amazing that David actually felt pretty good during the days he was unable to get the Gleevec chemo pills.

**We had to believe that all these things were
being used to work for His good
and to stretch our faith in our God who provides.**

-112-

January 2009

I called Dr. Brown's office to see if the CT scan could be done as soon as possible. His nurse called and got the appointment changed to Monday, January 26, 2009. David felt very weak and had problems walking even with my assistance. When we got home about 4:30 P.M., he went to bed for the rest of the day. On February 2, we had an appointment with Dr. Brown to get the results of the CT scan. He said there were tumors in the pelvic region and fluid buildup, apparently causing pressure and pain. We were aware of these problems because we could feel the tumors in the lower abdomen area and see the result of the water/blood build up.

Dr. Brown said what we already knew, surgery was not an option in David's case. He said radiation was a possibility, but we were concerned that radiation would damage the liver and David did not want to have that type of treatment. I had looked up possible drugs that were available for GIST, some of which were being tested overseas and some in the States. I asked Dr. Brown about using Tasigna made by Novartis or Adult Stem Cell therapy. He was opened to idea of using Tasigna after looking up the drug on his Blackberry but did not have information on Adult Stem Cells. Other ideas were discussed, but we were aware there was no real answer.

David decided he wanted to see another doctor at that point. On February 3, I called Dr. Gina D'Amato, a GIST research specialist, whose name I had found in one of the postings by a GIST patient on www.LifeRaft.com, an international web site for GIST patients that I interacted with often. When I called Crawford W. Long Hospital in Atlanta, I was told Dr. D'Amato was a Sarcoma specialist as well as three other doctors whose names were given to me by the receptionist at the hospital. She indicated the Gist specialists were either at Emory University Hospital or Winship Cancer Institute, both being a part of Crawford W. Long complex, but on different campuses. I posted her finding on the Life Raft web site to share with the other patients who might need the on-line information.

Wednesday, February 4, the person who had first told me about Dr. D'Amato sent me an email he received directly from the doctor herself. I emailed Dr. D'Amato and gave her David's medical history concerning his battle with GIST since the first diagnosis December 2001. God answered yet another prayer. Three hours later Angela, a representative from Emory University Medical Midtown, called to get some information. She wanted to set up an appointment for David to see Dr. D'Amato! I called David to ask if he was willing to see the doctor in Atlanta. He said to tell him the date for the appointment and give him time to pack! We laughed at his eagerness. He was encouraged by the contact I had made and the prompt response from the hospital personnel. In about an hour after that blessing, I received a personal email from Dr. D'Amato saying she would be happy to see David and gave me contact information for Joan, who was in charge of new patient appointments. I contacted Dr. Brown's office in Dothan and requested David's records be sent to Dr. D'Amato so an appointment could be set up. The records were mailed to the Atlanta office the next day and the appointment was made for February 24.

Prayers were being answered with more
and more confirmation
God was moving us to continue our quest
for David's care.

-*113*-

FEBRUARY 2009

On February 24, 2009, we met with an intern, two medical students, and Dr. D'Amato for consultation and an exam of David's pelvic area. During that consultation, I felt like we were in an episode of the TV program "House." The doctor talked with us and looked over the latest CT scan as the intern and students took notes. They had a conference in Dr. D'Amato's office after they met with us. Dr. D'Amato came back to the examination room where we were waiting and told us there were several types of chemo we could consider. She gave us three prescriptions for three separate types of chemo pills including Tasigna that I had asked about and told us to see which one was available with financial assistance for David's cancer treatment. The doctor told David to increase the 600 mg of Gleevec to 800 mg. Prior to 2008, the 800 mg dosage of Gleevec was prescribed overseas, but not in the US.

David started the increased dosage of the drug on the February 24. He began to have more weakness, dizziness, fatigue, and nausea after the first increased dosage. Later in the week, he began using a cane to help steady his steps. I contacted Novartis Pharmaceutical Company, maker of Gleevec and maker of the new drug, Tasigna. We had already been through the petitioning process in August 2008 to get Novartis' help with the cost of Gleevec. When the petition was turned down, I sent in the appeal asking for financial assistance for the chemo pills starting in September. Novartis had accepted us for coverage of Gleevec through September of 2009 for one year. We had been asked by Novartis to re-apply in December 2008 to have current paperwork on hand concerning taxable income for the last year taxes were filed. Therefore, it was to our advantage to get another Novartis chemo drug, if possible, assuming the drugs would be provided at little or no cost to us.

Of the three drugs suggested to us by Dr. D'Amato, Tasigna was her first choice, and from what I had read on the internet, I agreed that it appeared to be the best choice for treatment. Dr. Tom Brown, our Oncologist in Dothan, agreed it would be a good drug for David to "try" after checking the information on Tasigna. The data from clinical trials for Tasigna had indicated Leukemia patients using the drug had positive results from its use.

March- July 2009

At the next appointment with Dr. D'Amato two months later, she told us the increased dose of Gleevec was not showing signs of being effective. She suggested we try Tasigna and told us that drug, in her opinion, would help with the pelvic tumors. In the meantime, the blood in the scrotum was clearing up on its own as the Urologist in Dothan had predicted it would. Novartis representatives were contacted by me after David's appointment with Dr. Tom Brown in Dothan, March 2.

On March 3, I spoke with a representative who could not find the information concerning our coverage for Gleevec for the year. Each day that week, I called to see what had been worked out by the representatives at Novartis. On Friday, March 6, I was told the Tasigna chemo pills would be shipped to our home and the cost for the drug would be covered totally by Novartis through December of 2009.

God worked out all the red tape and the medicine arrived in the afternoon of March 10.

David was off the Gleevec for three days, per instructions by Dr. D'Amato, and started taking the Tasigna on Saturday, March 14. God gave us coverage for fifteen months due to the paperwork requirements for the new drug in 2009. It causes us to laugh with joy at His marvelous ways of working out these details on our behalf! David had slight side effects from Tasigna, but it appeared his pelvic tumors were beginning to shrink. He began to get weaker around May 15. Dr. Brown and Dr. Spence had mentioned David might want to consider Hospice care. He had not been ready to do so when they spoke to him at his prior appointments with them.

On May 15, I asked him to consider trying Hospice for a while and if he wanted to dismiss them, he could do so at any time. He agreed but was upset saying it looked like he was giving up by asking for this type of help. Covenant Hospice began sending a nurse to check David's vital signs three times a week, beginning on May 15. Our children, grandchildren, and friends from Marianna and Jacksonville came that weekend to see David because they were concerned he might pass away in a short time. To show the family he was determined to keep on living, he got up on Sunday, dressed and when I got home from church, told me we were taking the family out for lunch at the truck stop in town. God's grace and sheer determination kept him pushing forward.

David accepted Covenant Hospice care and in July allowed the nurse to bring oxygen for him to use. It was not imperative, but the nurse and I felt he could gain some benefit from its usage. He continued to work around the house as he had energy. He cleaned out the room that once was his office, did some work in the basement and on the grounds around our home. He had a fall one morning due to his foot going to sleep. He tried to stand and when he put weight on his left foot, he fell beside his lift chair, hitting the left side of his head on the corner of the fireplace in the living room, then landed on his bottom. A few days later, he fell coming up the back steps as he tried to bring in our flag from the mailbox post. He lost his balance on the second step and fell backward toward our van that was parked in the garage. The van broke his fall and he landed on his left knee.

On Thursday, July 16, David began to have burning pain in the pelvic tumors. The pain went through to his back. We called the Hospice nurse on duty who called the Hospice doctor, Dr. Spence.

He prescribed a pain pill for nerve pain called Gabapentin (600 mg), a generic for Neurontin. After two and a half days on the medicine, it began to control his pain but caused tremors. He could hardly feed himself because he could not control his hands by July 19.

I had prayed for Resurrection Power (the strongest power I knew about) on Sunday, the nineteenth, asking the Lord to help him feel much better and be able to go with Michael and me to Panama City the next day. I was to have my Pre-Op consultation and tests at the Urological Center where my surgeon, Dr. Eisenbrown, had her office. Then I was to go to the Bay Medical Center for paperwork and an EKG prior to surgery at the center on the July 21.

By Monday, July 20, David was much better and ready to go to Panama City with Michael and me. Casey, our ten-year-old grandson, also went with us to help his "grandparents." On Tuesday, Michael, Christy, Caleb (eleven) and Casey (ten) drove us to Bay Medical Center for my 11 A.M. appointment. Our friends, Mike Palmer, and his daughter, met us at the hospital and stayed with the family as I was prepared for surgery. The family was allowed to come back and visit with me a few minutes after the vitals were recorded in the computer and then I was taken to a waiting area, dressed in my hospital gown, to wait for the doctor to arrive. When the doctor came in I was taken to the Operating Room about 1:40 P.M.

The operation lasted about an hour. After coming out of surgery, I had to wait for a room to be cleaned and then was put in room 257 where the family was invited in to visit. I felt fine and had no pain. There was pressure in the bladder area when I was asked to move from side to side. David went back home Tuesday night to rest and Michael spent the night with him to be available if David needed anything. They had a restful night and the next day Michael, Christy, and David came over around lunch time to check me out of the hospital.

God had blessed us through the surgery and kept David strong enough to be with me during this time along with Michael's family. It was so meaningful to have family who stood by and were willing to help in any way they could.

OCTOBER 2009

In October of 2009, David and I went to Blairsville, Georgia, to spend some time in the mountains. He had to drop Hospice care in Marianna because we would be out of town for over two weeks. I contacted United Hospice of Blue Ridge, Georgia, so David could continue to be monitored with hospice care. On October 12, after two weeks under United Hospice, David had an appointment with Dr. D'Amato in Atlanta, about a two-hour drive. The doctor wanted David to have a PET scan. Therefore, he had to be taken off Hospice care in order for Medicare to pay for the scan. We dropped United Hospice and began home care with United Health Care of Blue Ridge, Georgia.

A nurse came out to infuse David with Saline Solution three times that week. We had David's blood count taken by the nurse a few days later. He was given two units of blood on October 24 at Union General Hospital in Blairsville due to his hemoglobin being 7.9. On October 26, David had a PET scan at Emory University Hospital, Atlanta. On October 29, David had an appointment with Dr. D'Amato. She could not find any pelvic tumors and told us the largest tumor in the liver seemed to be dying as well. That was the good news we had hoped to hear.

Dr. D'Amato prescribed Nexavar, a chemo pill made by Bayer Pharmaceuticals. He was to continue on Tasigna chemo pills until the Nexavar could be secured. I contacted Jayme Alfano to see if Aetna Medicare insurance he had researched and suggested for retirees of the Florida Baptist Convention, would provide coverage by November 1, 2009. If so, it would cover the $7,000 a month cost of the new chemo pills. From the information I had read in the material sent to us by Aetna, it appeared the company would cover two-thirds of the cost and the patient would have to pay the remaining 33 percent. Jayme checked with a representation from the insurance company and was told the drugs would be covered.

In a few weeks, a representative from Nexavar Reach Program told me the co-pay would be about $2,000 a month. I told the representative, in that case, David would need financial assistance in getting the meds. They needed the first page of the most recent income tax form with a letter stating why financial assistance was needed for the entire amount of the drugs. One week later, I was contacted by the representative and told the drugs would be sent to David for one year at no cost to him!

**Praise the Lord! He provided yet again and
met the need we laid before Him.**

-116-

TRIPS TO THE ER

On December 11, I took David to the ER at our local hospital with an intestinal blockage. He weighed about 130 pounds at the time. His stomach was pumped out for two days. On the third day, he was allowed to have liquids for two meals. The following day he was given solid food to eat. When all the systems were working properly, Dr. Spence allowed him to go home on December 15. The next day was my birthday. David had planned to take me out for dinner, so although he was weak, he told me he felt like going out that night. We drove out of town to a restaurant recommended by a Marianna friend and returned home after the meal. He slept all the way over to the restaurant and all the way home.

The next few days, he was fairly active. He packed his clothes, food items, and home health equipment to take to the mountains on our Christmas vacation. The morning of December 24, we had the van packed for a trip to our son's home in St. Mary, Georgia. David had gone to town to get his prescription for the month we planned to be in the mountains after sharing Christmas Eve and Christmas Day with Michael's family.

Our daughter, Michele, and her family were to come up to Blairsville from Jacksonville, so we could all be together. When David returned from town he told me he had stomach pain like he did on the eleventh and felt like he needed to go to the hospital. He was admitted on Christmas Eve and went through the same treatment as he did December 11-15. On December 29, Dr. Spence agreed to request Covenant Hospice to resume assistance for David per David's request. David was released later that day and told me he felt well enough to go out to eat lunch at the Chinese restaurant before going home. I was amazed he wanted to eat out, but we did and then went home for him to rest.

-117-

DAVID'S DECLINE

On the night of December 29, he was up five times and got very little rest. He seemed to have a reaction to a prescription sleeping medication he had been given by the specialist in Atlanta but had never used until that night. He wanted to try it and see if he could rest better than he had in the hospital. Due to the reaction, we realized he should not take it again. In the days following, he was weak and was not able to feed himself, would forget to chew or swallow, could not open his eyes fully, and would fall asleep if I did not call his name or try to keep him alert.

-118-

DAVID'S SIXTY-NINTH BIRTHDAY

I remember observing David during the week. He could not stay awake nor feed himself, for the most part. I prayed again for Resurrection power for David, so he could live to see his sixty-ninth birthday on January 25, 2010. Friends came by to visit him, assuming they were seeing him for the last time.

As the days drew nearer his birthday, I realized he was getting stronger and would love to celebrate the special day.

He had an appointment with Dr. Brown on January 25 in Dothan, AL. We planned to go out to eat at Cracker Barrel after the afternoon appointment. His blood work was done and the print out of the findings was given to us. The hemoglobin was 8.7, low enough to warrant a Procrit injection or a blood transfusion. We were aware that the Procrit infections for 2009 seemed to do little to bring up the count. David had a blood transfusion in the month of March ordered by Dr. Brown. In October while we were in Blairsville, GA he had another transfusion ordered by Dr. D'Amato, the GIST specialist from Emory University Hospital. As Dr. Brown looked over the numbers and talked with David about his condition, he told him he needed to get a transfusion of two units of blood. The choice was to go in the hospital immediately and have the transfusion at Flowers Hospital, adjacent to the Doctors Building where Dr. Brown had his office or wait and have the transfusion in

Marianna the next day. The decision was made to stay in Dothan and have the transfusion there.

Since David had wanted a Cracker Barrel meal, I offered to go and pick up a take-out order. He was hungry and eager for me to get him a birthday meal. He gave me a list of what he wanted to eat. I left the hospital and went to Cracker Barrel, ordered the take-out meals, and returned shortly thereafter. We enjoyed our meal as his transfusion began. After making a few calls to friends and family, updating them on his procedures, he went to sleep. I rested on the large couch in the hospital room and around 3:45 A.M. we were ready to drive the 45 miles back home.

-119-

RESURRECTION POWER

Prior to going in the hospital on December 11, we had made plans to go to the FL Worship Choir annual retreat January 28 and 29 in Daytona Beach, Florida. Even after going in the hospital, David continued to say he knew he would be better by the end of the month and would to be able to go on the trip by then. He looked so sick. I prayed Resurrection power over him as I had several times since May 2009 when he wanted to be at his Deaf student's graduation. He had interpreted for her for seven years. At that time, he had me call the student's mother the day before graduation to let her know he was too sick to attend. Her mother and I agreed to pray that he would be able to attend the service. The next day he was feeling strong enough to go as God had raised him for that special occasion, a definite miracle. Therefore I prayed He would lift David up one more time for the Daytona trip. God once again raised him up and the week we were to leave on the trip to Daytona Beach he was much stronger.

We drove 670 miles round trip staying with childhood friends of his while in the Daytona area. Our friends went to the concert with us on January 29, as we had prayed. God made it all come to pass. David was very tired and had to rest a lot during our trip, but was allowed by the Father to reach yet another goal in the strength of the Lord.

In January of 2010, we received a letter from Dr. D'Amato letting us know that she was resigning from her position at Emory University Hospital to go back in to research and other doctors would be taking her caseload. At that point, we requested David's records be sent from EUH to Dr. Brown in Dothan, so he could continue monitoring David's case.

-120-

ELEVENTH HOUR MEDICATION DELIVERY

On Monday, February 15, 2010, David counted out his chemo pills and realized he would be running out by Friday afternoon of that week. He asked me if I had heard from the Nexavar concerning a delivery date for his chemo. Each month since November 2009, a Nexavar representative had called to set up a delivery date a week or so prior to David needing the meds. I told him the representative had not called. The week before I had been contacted by letter from Nexavar Reach Program requesting we fill out paperwork for 2010 coverage of the meds. Enclosed in the letter was a form to be filled out by David in order for him to be considered for continued coverage for free chemo meds. I had filled in our portion of the form and faxed it to David's Oncologist, Dr. Brown, for him to complete the doctor's portion. Dr. D'Amato's name, address, and other information was on the printed form due to the fact she had written the original prescription for Nexavar in November 2009. Dr. Brown filled out one of the two sections of the paperwork, but failed to complete the second section. I called Nexavar Reach Program on February 16 to ask if they had received the paperwork from Dr. Brown. The representative I talked with said Dr. Brown had faxed in the paperwork that same day but had failed to indicate how many refills were allowed and at what dosage. I contacted Dr. Brown's nurse that afternoon and told her what information was needed on the form and that Nexavar would send the form back to Dr. Brown's office.

Due to the paperwork delays, the Nexavar representative told me that David might have to be without his chemo pills for a day or two while the information was received and reviewed by the committee for approval. She also asked that I called Cura Script Pharmacy on Wednesday to request immediate shipment of the medication that David needed by Thursday, February 18. We did not hear back from Nexavar as to whether we had approval for coverage of the meds or not, but I called Cura Script Pharmacy on Wednesday morning and requested the medicine be sent as soon as possible. The lady I spoke with told me the medication would be shipped to us at no cost, which indicated Nexavar Reach Program committee had decided to continue covering the expense of the drug for David. I checked to make sure the Cura Script computer records showed the correct dosage and refill schedule required before shipment so everything was in order. The prescription information was just as Dr. D'Amato had originally prescribed it.

**I told David I knew the Lord would provide the meds
even at the eleventh hour!**

When I asked when the meds would arrive, the pharmacist said on Thursday, February 18. The next day, UPS delivered the Nexavar chemo pills around 3:15 P.M. David had taken his last two pills at 4 A.M. that morning. The next dose was due at 4 P.M. The Lord provided the drugs, at the eleventh hour, on the day they were needed, 45 minutes before they were to be taken!

**What a blessing it was to see how He worked it all out
for our good!**

-121-

MY FALL

On February 25, 2010, I had a major fall at Idlewild Baptist Church, Tampa, Florida. About 350 singers and 50 orchestra members of the FL Worship Choir had met at IBC to make a CD for Prism Music company. After several hours of recording, we were given a break to put on our formal attire to have a professional picture made for the inside cover of the 2010 CD jewel case. The earbuds, FM radio, and music folder were bundled up in my arms as I took the first step into the aisle from the seventh row of the choir where I had been standing during the recording. There were no railings in the steep choir loft to hold on to for stability.

My foot slipped off the edge of the step and I fell backward toward the left side, falling down to the fourth and fifth rows as chairs tumble all around me. Several men who were close by hurried over to help get me up on my feet. I was still holding my music folder in my left arms as well as my FM radio, but the earbuds had flown through the air, landing several feet away. The first impact from the fall was on my right shoulder. That area toward the back, around the right arm, and down to the elbow began swelling. There was a fairly deep cut on the outside of the right arm and left shin. I hit my head on both sides, against the wooden chairs, hit my mid spine, and landed on my left hip. There was also a small skinned place on my right knee.

Two of the men in the choral group helped me up and I was able to walk down the steps with their assistance to the floor level of the sanctuary. A staff member at Idlewild Baptist Church provided First Aid and fill out the necessary forms due to the accident being on church property. When I got home after the two-day recording session, I had X-rays at my monthly chiropractic appointment. The chiropractor told me there appeared to be no broken bones or injuries, just bruises, and cuts. I had put ice on the major areas of discomfort the night of the accident, taken Aleve tablets, and later used moist heat for my sore muscles. My chiropractor adjusted my spine, neck, etc. three times the week following that appointment until I was feeling better. Once again, the devil tried to destroy me, but the Lord surrounded me by angels who took the blows that could have taken my life.

**God gave me another testimony to share
concerning His watch care over His beloved child.**

-122-

DAVID FALLS AGAIN

On May 11, David went to bed early and slept all through the night. The next day, I checked on him and saw that he was still asleep. Around 4 P.M. Tuesday afternoon, he was sleeping soundly so I did not wake him. Before I started to bed, I looked in on him again. He had attempted to get up and had fallen beside the bed. He could respond when I asked him questions but spoke with slurred speech. He appeared to be semi-conscious. I told him to stay on the floor and then I called 911.

The Emergency Medical Service workers arrived about 20 minutes later and checked to see if he had any broken bones. The man in charge told me he did not think there were bones broken but understood when I told him I preferred he go to the hospital to have X-rays taken. The men took David to the hospital in the EMS vehicle. I gathered up his billfold and other items we needed and drove to the hospital getting there just after the EMS vehicle had parked at the ER entrance. X-rays were taken and three hours later the doctor on duty told us there were no broken bones. We were free to go home. The same men who brought David into the hospital took him back to our house and I met them there.

David decided to sleep in his lift chair in the living room that night. I asked him to blow the whistle he had around his neck on a cord if he had to get up during the night. He agreed to do so, but later he decided to move the whistle to a chair nearby. When he woke up and needed to go to the bathroom, he could not find the whistle in the darken room, so he tried to walk to the nearest bathroom by himself. He got confused and fell into the tub, cutting his elbows and arms. It is a miracle that he was not hurt worse and got out of the tub by himself.

God was there to help him again.

He washed off the blood as best he could and went back to sleep in the lift chair. When I got up to give him his regular pain meds about an hour later, I found the evidence of the fall and injuries. I cleaned up the blood off the sink area and left the other evidence for the hospice aide to see and clean up when he came the next day. I found David's whistle and had him put it around his neck where he could not lose it, bandaged up his wounds, and gave him the pain meds. We went back to sleep for the night.

We praised the Lord once more for no broken bones.

The next day when the Hospice nurse came to check on him I told her what had happened. David was very upset as he heard the details and told me he did not remember the falls nor any of the things that had happened. God protected him with ministering angels to keep him from being hurt worse. The Hospice aide came later and cleaned up the blood from the shower curtain, bathtub, and helped David with his shower.

-123-

DAVID'S FALL IN JUNE

June 14-16, 2010, Michele and her three children came for a visit from Jacksonville. She also brought Michael's boys with her, so the cousins could all enjoy being together for a few days and we could be with all five our grandchildren at one time. I had an appointment with my chiropractor on the sixteenth and left Michele and the children in charge of watching over David. I had been in the doctor's office about fifteen minutes and been called back to the treatment room when David called me on my cell phone. He told me he had fallen in the bathroom, hit his head on the Jacuzzi tub, and injured his arm. He was in pain and wanted to go to the hospital for X-rays. When I returned home from the doctor's office about thirty minutes later, with Michele's help and the children doing what they could to get David into the van, I drove us to the hospital. He was given an injection for pain and X-rays were taken. A few hours later, the attending doctor told us there were no broken bones, but the cancer had spread to the shoulder, therefore was in the bones. We were not surprised the cancer had spread.

**We were thankful to the Lord that once again
David had not broken bones.**

A sling was put on the arm for support and we went back home. He ate lunch and then went to bed. We put ice on the shoulder for the remainder of the day. The next day, we applied heat to the shoulder. The Hospice nurse came by to check on David on Wednesday. He was in pain when he moved, but when he took his regular pain medication and remained stationary he was able to sleep.

We praised the Lord and were amazed at His constant care over David's frail body.

-124-

ROOF CLEANERS

As I was walking to the mailbox on Thursday morning, I noticed the leaves had collected on the roof of our house and thought to myself, "I need to ask someone to come clean off the roof." Later in the afternoon, there was a knock on our front door. Tommy, a deacon from our church, came in to visit and asked if he and some of the men on his team could clean off the roof and do any other jobs around the house for us. I told him about my thinking that morning we needed to have the roof cleaned off. He said the Ministry team could come on Saturday, so the plans were made for them to minister to us. God provides for every moment of every day. What a blessing!

He meets our needs even before we would think to ask.

SITTERS PROVIDED

Getting sitters to be with David was a challenge, but I made a list of neighbors and friends who had told me they were willing to come if needed. We had a list of friends we had used in the past with three of our parents, so I updated the list and made some calls. One neighbor, a retired nurse, came when I went to my regular appointments with my chiropractor. Other neighbors picked up groceries for me. My backyard neighbor sat on Wednesday nights, so I could go to choir rehearsal. A friend who had worked for us several years at Blue Springs Baptist Assembly and her grandson who worked at the local hospital, came on Sundays so I could be in my place in the choir for the morning service. She had Sunday afternoon services, so she was available during the time we had our church services.

The sitters had been coming on time and everything was working out until the last Wednesday night in June when my scheduled sitter did not come. I called her and she told me she was not aware I needed her that night and had not planned to come. Evidently, we had a communication problem since I thought she realized I needed her each Wednesday in June. I prayed about the situation, called the choir director to tell him about the problem, and asked him to send someone to sit for me who might be leaving Prayer Meeting that night. If no one came, I would know it was God's will for me to stay with David. No one came.

-126-

KATHY

July 4 was the next time I needed a sitter and started calling friends a week in advance to see who I could get to come be with David while I was at church that morning. My regular Sunday sitter could not come due to special services at her church. My back-up sitter was going to be out of town. I prayed about whom I should call and the Lord impressed on me to call Kathy, a former worker at Blue Springs Baptist Assembly where David had been Manager and I was Secretary for over eighteen years. The challenge was that I had not heard from her in about two years and did not know if she still lived in the area.

Mary, one of my choir friends, knew Kathy so I called Mary and asked her how to contact Kathy. I had looked in the phone book but did not see her listed. Mary said she would make some calls and see what she could find out. I called Kathy's sister-in-law who told me she had not heard from Kathy in a long time. She told me to call her husband's cell phone and see if he knew where Kathy was. When I talked with him, he told me the same thing his wife did, that he had not heard from her since her husband died.

As I continued to pray, I knew the Lord would take care of my needs as He saw fit. I was content to rest in Him and see what He would work out for me. The next morning, Kathy called and told me she heard that I wanted to contact her. We had a brief time of catching up and she said she would be glad to sit with David on Sunday or any other time I needed her. My Wednesday night sitter was going to be out of town July 7, so I asked Kathy to come that night also. She agreed.

**God worked it all together for our good
and it was a blessing to connect once again with Kathy**.

-127-

TRANSFUSION AND CONFERENCE TO FOLLOW

In September, I asked the Hospice nurse who came to our home twice a week to take David's vital signs to also check his hemoglobin. David and I knew that the count must be low due to his weak condition. The count was 8.7 which qualified him for a blood transfusion under Medicare guidelines. We had been told during David's illness, that if the count was ten or above Medicare would not pay for the transfusion. He became weaker in the month that followed. I asked a week or so later that the blood work be done and the Hospice nurse took another sample to be processed at the lab. We were called and were told the count was 7.8, continuing to go down.

The Hospice doctor sent word that it was "inappropriate" for David to have another transfusion. David had a transfusion in October 2009 at Union General Hospital, another transfusion in January 2010 at Flowers Hospital on his birthday, and a transfusion in March of 2010 at Union General Hospital. We realized the pattern showed that the transfusions were of little help, but David wanted all the help he could get. After we discussed what David wanted to do concerning the transfusion, we decided to contact his Oncologist, Dr. Brown to get an appointment the next week and have blood work done by his nurse. When Dr. Brown saw the hemoglobin count was 8.3, he wrote an order for a blood transfusion and sent us to Flowers Hospital. The transfusion was begun about 6:00 P.M. on Thursday, September 23, 2010, and the second unit of blood was administered around 9:30 P.M. The process was completed at 1:30 A.M. on Friday, September 24. He felt good that day and was discharged around 11:30 A.M.

We did some shopping, stopped at the TCBY yogurt shop, had lunch, and drove back to Marianna. When we arrived in Marianna, David wanted to run some errands and order a take-out meal from a health food store that had been expanded to include a delicatessen. We left the deli and went to Wal-Mart to buy some groceries and got home about 5:00 P.M., a rather full day for someone who had just gotten out of the hospital!

Saturday and Sunday, David had very little energy. He did not feel like going to church and stayed home to rest. Monday, he felt stronger and we continued to make plans to go out of town for my high school class reunion in Pembroke, Georgia, on October 2 and onto Blairsville, on October 3. While in the mountains, we also had plans to meet a group of senior adults from our church to attend the David Jeremiah conference from October 17-21, if David continued to feel like going. In faith, we had pre-paid for the event the middle of September.

God sent the amount needed for the conference the week we decided to go which was a confirmation we should continue with the desire of our hearts to attend.

-*128*-

THE CHECK FOR THE TRIP

Jim, a friend of ours from, Florida, contacted me by email the week before we were to leave for Blairsville. He wanted to ask about our mountain house and the possibility of renting it out for a week in November. We had not rented it before. Only our family had stayed in the house except for our son's pastor and wife when they brought a choir group for a week in October of 2009 to witness to tourists in the area. One of David's cousins and his wife had also spent part of a week in the house and left us a donation to take care of utilities.

David and I discussed the possibility of Jim and his wife spending a week at the house and emailed him to let him know it would be available for them. Jim emailed me and asked a few questions and also said he would send money to pay the housekeeper who cleaned for us as well as help with the cost of utilities as David's cousin had done. Two days before we were to leave on our trip, I had written a list of things I needed to do in town on Thursday. One of the main items on my list was going to the bank to get cash for the trip. On a previous trip to the mountains, I had taken more cash than we needed, so I had decided to only take out $300.00 for the month since I would use my Debit card for gas and other purchases.

Jim emailed me on Wednesday to let me know he was sending a check by a friend of his who was from Marianna and was at a meeting with him that day. I had no idea what time the gentleman would arrive. Around 2 P.M., I decided to check the mail to see if some pictures I had ordered had come and look over the bills that might be in the mailbox. As I was taking the mail out of the box, a car pulled up and asked for the McCormick residence. I realized that he must be Jim's friend who was bringing me the check. I told him my name and that I thought he had a check for me from Jim. He gave me the check and asked how David was doing. I invited him in to see David, but he said he was tired from his day of meetings and travel and had to get home so he could rest.

Walking back to the house with the day's mail and the check, I began to smile and said to the Lord, "I know this check must be for about $300.00. I just know you have provided once again, the exact amount we need for the trip." When I got in the house I sat down and opened the envelope from Jim. The check was for $300.00.

-129-

THE 2010 OCTOBER TRIP

We prayed we would be able to go my High School class reunion and then to Blairsville for the remainder of the month. All this depended on the Lord giving David the strength to do so. As the time got closer for us to make the trip, David continued to feel better each day. Our friend Billy provided a place for us to stay in his home as he normally did when we were in my home town after our home place had been sold. My brother, Buddy, from Savannah, came to see us at Billy's house the day of the reunion.

Later that day, we went to the Black Creek Golf Course Restaurant to meet with former high school friends for the reunion meal. Some of them had been in my classes from first grade through twelfth. David was able to go to the supper and stay for the recognition that followed but went to sleep during the meeting because he was so weak and had to take so many pain medications.

Sunday, we drove to Blairsville. We called United Hospice of Blue Ridge and asked that they cover David's care during the month we were in North Georgia. The nurses came about once or twice a week and checked on him. On October 11, he insisted I let him walk to the swing in the yard without my assistance. Normally I walked along beside him. He was gone about 15 minutes. I walked out of the house to check on him and could not see him near the swing. I called his name and when he answered I realized he was trying to come up the steps to the porch. He had fallen coming up the steps in the yard in front of the house, falling on his face, right shoulder, knees, and legs. I called the Hospice nurse and told her we needed lots of bandages since I did not have enough supplies on hand to bind up his wounds. She came to the house in about an hour, cleaned up the wounds, and bandaged the places that still were bleeding. It looked as though he might not get to go to the David Jeremiah Celebrators Conference October 17-21 in Sevierville, Tennessee, the cost of which we had prepaid. He was determined to go and almost cried when he thought there was a chance he might not heal enough to attend. He continued to get stronger for the six days that followed.

We decided to buy a roll-about walker with a seat, so he could rest in case there was a lot of walking involved when we got to the civic center. We drove three hours on October 17 and met the Joy Club members from Marianna who came up together on a chartered bus. We stayed in the Holiday Inn with the Marianna group. Each day we would ride on the bus to the civic center with our friends, go out to lunch with them afterward, and do some sightseeing. After the first day, we realized this schedule would allow little time for David to rest. Our pastor and his family had brought their vehicle to Sevierville, so they could join us for the conference. Since he had his own car, we asked him to take us back to the motel for the following afternoons.

We joined the group on the bus around 4:30 P.M. each day to ride back to the night meetings, which meant we did not get back to the motel until after 10 P.M. The group always wanted to go out to eat on the way back to the motel since there was little time to eat before the conference. David was given the strength to make the trip, sleeping wherever he was as best he could, whether during the meetings or on the bus or at the motel. It was an answer to prayer that he had the energy to keep going.

God gave us another miracle, indeed.

-130-

FL Baptist Convention Annual Meeting Surprise Interpreter

The FL Baptist Worship Choir was invited to sing at the FL Baptist Convention Meeting at First Baptist Church in Brandon, Florida, on Tuesday, November 9. In faith, I had made reservations for us for November 8, hoping David would feel well enough to make the trip. David decided on Saturday, November 6, he also wanted to attend the Church Music Conference that was held at Bell Shoals Baptist Church in Brandon on November 8, so we had to change our plans and arrive several hours earlier in order to be at the 1:00 P.M. meeting. After that meeting was over, we checked in the motel and went out to eat supper. It was too late for us to get to First Baptist Church for the beginning of the first session of the convention meeting at that point, although David wanted to try to make it, so we went back to the motel to rest.

David told me he wanted to attend all the meetings on Tuesday. I was amazed he was going to push himself to attempt to be in the sessions from 8:30 A.M. until we attended the 5:00 P.M. annual dinner given for the retirees of the FL Baptist Convention. Since there was no room for all 350 members of the FL Worship Choir to sing in the choir loft, only 100 of us were notified by email to sing at the event. I realized it was a miracle of God's grace that I was invited. I had to be on the stage with our group at 12:00 P.M. Tuesday, so when the morning session let out for lunch, David and I got a take-out order from a restaurant near the church, ate in the van, and then David took a nap while I went to the rehearsal.

He attended the 1:20 P.M. convention session and stayed until the dinner meeting was over that night. We got back to the motel around 7:00 P.M. He was very tired but glad he had the energy to attend the meetings and see so many of our friends from around the State of Florida, many of whom had prayed for him daily.

God blessed us in amazing ways to help us have such a perfect trip. Most of the time, David said he felt good although he would fall asleep from time to time due to his weakened condition. We had perfect weather and no problems with our vehicle. We thank God for helping us take part in the worship and fellowship time at the convention meetings. We knew it could be the last time we would get to attend the annual meeting together.

I was called November 17, 2010, by one of our interpreters who works with Hannah, a Deaf student at Marianna High School, and asked if I could substitute for her that day since she was sick. While Hannah and I were walking to her afternoon class, we stopped and talked with Bob, a Deaf employee at the school. We visited a few minutes before going to class. I invited both of them to come to church on Sunday. They had come a few times in the past, but not on a regular basis. Bob said he could not because he had to work. I told him he needed Jesus and needed to be at church. He nodded.

Hannah said she wanted David to come to school, so she could see him. I told her to come to church and she could see him there. On November 21, 2010, David and I were at our church for Sunday School and the morning worship service as was our custom. After the music worship service, the pastor began preaching. The Interpreter for the Deaf at our church received a texted message from Hannah and Bob that week, telling her that they could not come to church because Bob had to work. The interpreter had planned to sing in the choir and then be available to interpret the sermon if any Deaf came to the service. Her daughters both became sick just before she was to leave home to come to church, so she did not get to attend.

During the sermon, I looked up from the choir loft where I was sitting and there was Hannah and Bob coming down the aisle. The two of them came down to the front of the church and sat on the first row. I got Hannah's attention and signed to her that David was in the service. At that point, I did not know if he saw them come in or not. Many times he sat in the back of the church in case he did not feel well enough to stay and sometimes waited for me in our van until the service was over. However, that day he was sitting about three rows back from the front on the same side of the church where the Deaf sat. He was alert enough to notice them come in and realized no interpreter was present. At that point, he walked down the aisle, asked for a chair to be brought in for him, knowing he was too weak to stand and interpret, and he began signing the sermon.

Larry, one of the choir members, noticed the Deaf come in and left the choir to ask his wife to come interpret for them. She was on standby each week in case our main interpreter could not come for some reason, but she also worked in the nursery on Sunday mornings unless she knew any of the Deaf were coming to church. The pastor turned around just before he saw David coming down the aisle with an expression on his face as to whether Larry or I saw the Deaf and if we could take care of the situation. Someone told me he had gone to the nursery to get his wife to interpret. I indicated to the pastor that everything was being taken care of, so he continued to preach.

As Amy came into the auditorium from the nursery, she noticed David was already signing for the Deaf. She sat down on the front row with Hannah and Bob as David continued communicating the Gospel message as the pastor spoke. Each of us involved in the Deaf ministry were watching to see if David would step aside and let Amy relieve him, but he signed for the remainder of the service, even when one of the deacons was asked to present the budget for 2011.

It was amazing to watch as God gave David the alertness and energy to be used in such a marvelous way. The deacon who was to present the budget for a vote opened his remarks by saying how touched he was as he watched David "do that." The pastor added, "We have seen the sermon today." His sermon topic had been about commitment to service and ministry.

**God used David as an example of an available servant
being given His strength
to minister to those with special needs.**

-131-

Home-Going

We had planned to go to the mountains of Blairsville, December 26, 2010, and meet our children and grandchildren there, hoping to stay a few days with them during the Christmas holidays, as we had done in years passed when David felt well enough. All these plans were in God's hands and we continued to pack clothes and get ready for the trip. On December 23, David told me he would like to go to Wal-Mart and do some shopping. We had not shopped for Christmas, but I had put a few small things in gift bags and placed them under our Christmas tree a week before. David said he was having a good day and wanted to get out for a while. He took his rolling walker out of the back of the van without my help when we reached the parking lot at Wal-Mart.

After about two hours of shopping, not finding the items he was looking for, we paid for our groceries and started home. Across the street, he saw Beef O Brady's Restaurant and said he thought he might want to eat there. I did not think he felt like going because the walk around Wal-Mart had drained him of the little energy he had, but the restaurant was new in town and he wanted to know what kind of food they had. I started to drive in that direction and he said he had changed his mind and thought he needed to go home and rest.

When we got home he had a snack, laid down in his hospital bed to watch TV, and promptly went to sleep. We were only up once during the night, so we both were both blessed with a good night's rest. The next morning, December 24, David woke up feeling very weak. When he came into the kitchen where I was sending an email, I could tell it was a very bad day for him by the way he looked.

He told me, "I feel so bad."

He seemed surprised because he had such a good day on Thursday. Through the years, this had happened many times. He could have a good day and then the next day he was in bed and could not eat. A few days later, he would be ready to go on another trip. We often said he was "being healed" on days when he felt good. He agreed and would say, "I hope so."

He asked me to make him a piece of toast but did not feel like eating anything else. He sat in his lift chair and I noticed he was taking off his shirt. He usually was cold and even on days when the outside temperature was 70 degrees or so, he wanted a small heater turned on next to where he sat or near the bed where he lay down. When I brought the toast for his breakfast, he took off his undershirt, telling me he was too warm. Then he asked me to turn on the ceiling fan.

After he ate, he put a blanket around his shoulders and dosed off to sleep. Two hours later, he woke up and told me he was having a lot of pain and needed his scheduled pain meds early. I gave him the pain pills and he went back to sleep. His breathing became labored although he was on oxygen. I could see his pulse in his neck throbbing rapidly. Since this was a change from the norm, I called the Covenant Hospice nurse on duty for the holidays and she came out to check his vital signs in about 30 minutes. I told her which pain meds he had and she charted the information in her computer. Then she said if we needed her again to call. About thirty minutes after the nurse left, I called Lori, a retired nurse who lived down the street from us and asked that she check his temperature. Our thermometers were not working properly, but I knew he had fever. Lori came in a few minutes, took the temperature and found it to be 102 degrees. She charted the information on a tablet for me, gave him a 325 mg aspirin and left the thermometer with me to use during the weekend. I checked his temperature every few hours, gave him additional aspirin, but it remained 102 degrees. The temperature began to go down on Saturday noon. At that point, I told him he was doing better.

Even with oxygen, his breathing was still rapid and he said he had a minimal benefit from the aid. His labored breathing continued throughout the day and into Sunday. He used his walker to get back and forth from the bathroom but needed me to steady his steps. His system apparently started shutting down and bodily functions were being stressed to the maximum. His pain was acute even with his regular pain medications being taken at the scheduled times on Sunday.

I began giving him .5 mg of liquid morphine from the Hospice Comfort Pack around 4 p.m. Every two hours, I gave him an additional .5 mg which was the amount suggested by the Hospice nurse a few months before when we had to use it for the first time to help him get relief. After the third dose of liquid morphine, I called the Hospice nurse to let him know how David's condition was changing. The nurse arrived about 40 minutes later and observed the situation. He gave David another .5 mg of the morphine and waited 15 minutes to see if David felt any relief. He asked David if he felt any better.

As he gasped for breath, David said it might have helped minimally, but then said, "Not really."

The nurse gave him another .5 mg of morphine and waited again to see if that would help. I knew it was dangerous to continue giving him more morphine. He asked David again if his pain had decreased. David said it had not. He cried out in pain every few minutes. The nurse realized he could not do anything else, so he left, telling us to call if there was any change. About midnight, David went back to the bathroom, but his system was not functioning. The edema in his feet and stomach had continued to get worse over a period of weeks and he was bloated. The fluids may have gone to his heart as his doctor had told us he was concerned it would. The fluid pills he had taken about two weeks helped to a certain extent, but fluid continued to build up.

When David decided to go back to bed, he wanted to sleep in the hospital bed at the foot of our king size bed. During the earlier part of the night, he had slept in his lift chair in the living room where he normally was fairly comfortable. He lay down in the hospital bed, cried out in pain several times but finally was quiet. I assumed he went to sleep at that point. We both rested well during the night until I got up about 6 a.m. to go to the bathroom.

I checked his chest to see if he was breathing as I had done for nine years when I watched him sleeping. The chest was motionless. I knew he was "gone." I felt his hands. They were cold. I felt his tummy and it was warm, so I knew he must have died between 5 and 6 a.m. The procedure at that point was to call Hospice and let the nurse on duty know about the death.

I identified myself and then told him, "I think David is no longer with us."

He seemed a bit surprised and said he would come immediately. It took him about 45 minutes to get to the house. In the meantime, I sat on the bed beside David and held his cold hand.

I asked him, "David, did you die in your sleep?"

I smiled and then said, "I think you died in your sleep as we prayed you would."

I realized that the peace we had through the nine years of his terminal illness continued to cover me. I knew he was with the Father.

The scripture tells us when we are absent from the body we are present with the Lord.

-*132*-

FUNERAL PLANS

Our pastor called to check on us on Monday about an hour after David died. I had sent messages out to his wife and other friends on Sunday night, telling them David was having problems breathing and had a rapid heartbeat. The pastor told me he was out of town for the holidays with his family visiting his wife's folks, therefore, he would not be back in Marianna in time for the funeral. I was aware of that and assured him that was fine and I had planned to use two of David's cousins, ordained ministers, to officiate at the funeral. At that point, I called David's cousin Gwenn, from Morriston, Florida, and his cousin, John, from Lake City, and asked them if they were available to take part in the service. Gwen said he would be glad to and would call me later for details after I had planned the program.

John, however, told me he was not sure his boss would let him off work because John and one other worker who had similar responsibilities on the job had to share duty. The other man was off work for the holidays and John was supposed to be on duty until his co-worker got back. I told John I would pray he could either take part on the program for the funeral on Thursday in Marianna or at the graveside service on Friday in Jacksonville. He called me back on Tuesday to tell me he could not get off but could be at the service on Friday. I told him I knew God would work things out the way He had planned and we would be glad to have him speak on Friday along with our son-in-law, Jerry, who was also an ordained minister.

Just as I finished the call to John on Tuesday, my daughter told me our pastor from First Baptist Church, Marianna, had called while I was at the funeral home and left word to have me call return his call. He told me he felt like he should come back for the funeral. He was concerned that the members of our family and our church would wonder where he was at a time of great need in our family. I assured him we understood he was out of town for the holidays and I had other ministers in our family who could serve at the funeral. He asked me if he could have a prayer or do something for us at the funeral if I could use him. It was as though the Lord was telling me that was why John could not come and he had touched the heart of our pastor showing him he needed to be with us. I told him he could read the obituary, the scripture, and close with prayer.

The Lord worked out the speakers in just a matter of moments that day. Our pastor made an interesting observation concerning the timing of David's home-going. The Florida Baptist Convention voted in their annual meeting in November 2010 to sell Blue Springs Conference Center, a place we had called home for over eighteen years. We had been privileged to attend the two-day annual meeting when the decision was made to sell the conference center and other Baptist owned facilities due to the economic conditions in our country. The pastor mentioned that David was called home to heaven just a month later. The building of the conference center was completed in 1981. David was called to be Manager of the center in 1982. Dr. Harold Bennett, the Executive Director of the Florida Baptist Convention in the early 1980s had been instrumental in securing the land and helping committees make plans for the building of the Adult assembly.

In the 1960s, Dr. Bennett, had worked at the Home Mission Board in Atlanta when I was a secretary at that organization. He was speaking at the Baptist College of Florida in Graceville at a graduation that we attended after we had moved to Marianna. I made a special effort to wade through the crowd at the end of the meeting so I could speak to him. When he found out David and

I were in leadership at the assembly, he was thrilled. His dream became a reality and someone he loved was overseeing that special place! We had no doubt God had called us to work at the facility. From time to time as I welcomed guests at the registration desk, I was told, "We know God brought you here. You were meant to do this job." I often told them that I believed God built Blue Springs Conference Center just for us to share with them. It was a place of service where God had prepared us to live, work, and witness to thousands of people from the United States and other countries who attended the conferences held on those grounds. Now the time had come to an end for the conference center and David was being called to his eternal home.

-133-

THE CELEBRATION OF DAVID'S HOME-GOING

Thursday, December 30, I met with Chris Sikes, funeral director, at First Baptist Church with a program I had typed on the computer. He wanted everyone involved in the service to have a written program so there would be no confusion as to the order in which they would participate. Our family arrived a few minutes later. The pianist and organist I had asked to play pre-service music were to begin playing at 9:40 a.m. I wanted to hear the wonderful music they had prepared according to the list of musical selections David had asked to be used. Chris said he thought I might say that, so he told me just to go in whenever I wanted to. Instead of entering at 10:00 a.m., our family went in as the music began and sat on the front row on the piano side of the church.

Michael visited with friends throughout the church as Michele and her family sat with me. His wife came to the front row to wait for him to finish talking with many people he wanted to see before the service. At 10 a.m., all the family was in place on the front row. The Minister of Music came to the front row and bent down to talk to me. He said that our friend Royce had been out of town for the holidays, but had come home the night before. Royce had the power point presentation ready to be shown, as I had requested. He had produced the power point with information and pictures he had secured from me for recognition of David's Christian service vocation which was used at the Thanksgiving service where he was honored.

The power point was shown originally on November 22, 2009, at which time Royce had wanted David to lead our choir in several selection, play the organ for the service, and ring handbells. David was not physically able to conduct or play the instruments at the recognition service but was able to attend. I had asked that the presentation be shown at the funeral and God had arranged for Royce to come back from Christmas vacation just in time to provide the DVD to be used in the service. The Minister of Music reminded me that it was 15 minutes long and asked if I wanted to have the media personnel "run" it. I said, "Yes." He asked when I wanted it shown and I said at the first of the service. He let the man in the media booth know to start the DVD and the presentation began. After the power point presentation, there were two vocal solos by our former Minister of Music accompanied by his wife. There were two speakers, our pastor and David's cousin Gwenn. The pianist and organist each played selections David had requested as instrumental solos, one vocal solo presented, four congregational hymns were sung, two handbell selections were played by former ringers who had played under David's direction when he was Interim Minister of Music at First Baptist Church, Marianna, and a recording of me singing "His Eye is on the Sparrow" was played as David had requested. I am sure it was one of the longest funeral services most of the Baptist folks had every experienced, but I had told them in advance we were going to have lots of music.

Our Deaf friends from the local schools came and one of our interpreters signed the service for them. It was a glorious service! At the end of the service, Chris, the funeral director, escorted me to the Family Life Center where a meal was to be served for our family, our pastor, Gwen, the pallbearers, the organist, the pianist, and others who took part in the service. Most of the people who attended the service did not come over to the other building, so we missed seeing many of them. Several friends did come by and shared hugs and words of encouragement. It was a joyful experience and a true celebration of life, one of the most spirit-filled services I have ever witnessed! Michele and her family had to leave before the meal to get back to Jacksonville for our granddaughter's doctor's appointment. Michael and his family left with me about two hours later after I had packed for the trip to Kingsland, Georgia, where he and his family lived.

-134-

THE GRAVE SIDE SERVICE

Friday, December 31, the last day of the year, we left Kingsland and drove to Jacksonville for the graveside service at Greenlawn Cemetery. We were the first to arrive. The funeral director and his assistant met us and went over some questions they had for me. It was a beautiful day, cold but with lots of sunshine, just as the day of the funeral had been. A crowd of approximately 75 people began to gather. The funeral director was amazed so many people attended. He said normally there were only a few people at those type services. He said it spoke well of David and of our family. David's cousin, John, and our son-in-law, Jerry, spoke and led in prayer. In attendance were friends from both churches where David had served on staff in Jacksonville, two friends from the Deaf community, two interpreters who came to interpret for the Deaf (as God had provided for every need), two workers who had been on staff at Blue Springs Conference Center before their retirement who had also been to the funeral in Marianna, two friends from my home town in Georgia, David's High School friends who had kept in touch through the years, especially after he was diagnosed with a terminal illness, and others we had not seen in years.

After a brief service, we visited with people who remained and then we went to Jerry's parent's home for a meal. The fellowship was great and that same peaceful spirit filled the house as we enjoyed eating together. When we finished eating I road back to Kingsland, Georgia with Michael's family and we took much-needed naps. All of us were tired from the three-day planning and carrying out of the details for David's home-going and we needed some rest. Friday night, Michael got out a box of pictures David had given him when he was working on family tree information. We tried to identify the pictures that did not have names written on the back and had a good time telling stories of events remembered in David's life and that of his parents and grandparents. We could not identify all the people in the pictures but decided to talk with other family and friends when we could get together and see if they could help identify them.

What a sweet time of fellowship we had sitting there in the living room content in the Lord.

-135-

DAVID'S VISIT

A few weeks after David died, he visited me in a dream. He was dressed in his red and black checked shirt, the one he wore in a picture he had made when he worked at Malone School. In the dream, he came over to my side of the bed and kissed me on the forehead as I was waking up. There were no words spoken, but as happens in dreams sometimes, I understood the message he was giving me. He was telling me that our son, Michael and his family had come to our home to give us a surprise visit. I looked out the window of the bedroom which was not in the place where the window actually was located, and I could see Michael's vehicle. It was a pale green Suburban, not anything like the vehicle they actually had. David was letting me know that the family had just come in the house. I never saw anyone but David, yet I knew the family was somewhere in the house. He and I smiled at each other. The dream ended at that point.

What a lovely visit the Lord sent to me.

-136-

VISIT AT THE CHAPEL

While leaving Chipola College after subbing for the Deaf interpreter one afternoon, I had a desire to stop and see the little chapel on the grounds that had been recently built. I told the Lord if there was a parking place near the chapel, I would stop in and look around. When I got to the front of the chapel, I saw two parking places. I parked and went in to look around. It was small but had adequate seating for twenty or thirty people. When I went to the altar area, I noticed a large opened Bible. I wondered which section of scripture I would find. What a blessing to find my favorite scripture there before me from Proverbs the third chapter. I read the verses and thanked the Lord for bringing me there that day and to confirm His leadership as I read my favorite verses.

Does He really care about these little things in life? He does in my life and I am sure He does in yours. Why do we not naturally worship the God who sends us miracle after miracle and guides each step we take? He knows our thoughts before we think them. Isn't it interesting that in our modern society we have seminars to emphasize "learning how to worship." Worship happens when the worshipper is overcome with the grace of God shown to him or her and instantly gives Him the glory and falls before Him in gratitude that God is "mindful of him."

In Psalm 8:4-5 the author asks, "What is man that you are mindful of him?" We see the answer from scripture. We are "the apple of His eye, crowned with glory and honor, made a little lower than the angels for His good pleasure." Not only that, but He laid down His life to save us from sin, rose victorious from the grave, rewards us as we put our faith in Him, chooses to live through us, and gives us abundant life.

How amazing is our God!

I heard someone say, if we do not desire sin then everything we do is worship. I like enjoying fellowship with the God of the Ages, as the hymn writer declared, "O God, our help in ages past, our hope for years to come, our helper He amid the storm, and our eternal home." How can we hold back the worship? It just pours out as natural as breathing the breath of life He has breathed into us. God has taught me that worship is like breathing out. He breathes into us the breath of life and we become living souls. We breathe out that breath in worship. Our fitting response to Him is "Thank You, Lord!"

Recently I heard it said that the one thing we cannot do is refuse to breathe. Is it possible that we can refuse to worship? If that is the case, may God have mercy on us for not doing what should be natural for us as worshippers. I pray we will not worship the lesser things the world has to offer, but look to the Author and Finisher of our faith and stay before His throne daily, moment by moment, until we see Him in His glory.

We must be wise and listen to Him. Men can make demands on us. Their voices cry out loud for our attention. It is wise to listen for the "still small voice of the Lord." When we do listen to His voice, He will give us discernment in choosing where to go and what to do as one of His children.

April 30, 2011, I returned home from a two-day trip to Brandon, Florida, to sing with the Florida Worship Choir. Before pulling in my driveway, I stopped at the mailbox to pick up my mail. There was a bill from the phone company for $42.89 and a refund check for $50.00 from Patient's First saying I had overpaid my bill. Again,

I saw the hand of God blessing me. I smiled, bowed my head and said, "Thank You, Lord."

These daily miracles are expressions of His love.
What a blessing it is to receive them and
give Him the credit for what He chooses to do for me!

On May 4, 2011, as I contemplated the means to purchase a double bronze marker for David's grave and mine, so I could pay for it in advance of my death, I received a call from a company wanting to sell my timeshare in Kissimmee. I had tried for years to sell the property, but each company would require an up-front fee to advertise and there was no result in property sold. After hearing the representative present credentials and asking me to send almost $1,000 for the company to list the two weeks I "owned," I politely told the lady, "Even if I had $1,000.00 in my hand, right now, I would not send you the money. You are just a voice on the phone. Sorry." She tried to get me to reconsider my decision, but after that attempt, she ended the call.

September of 2011, I was in St. Petersburg, Florida to attend a rehearsal with the Florida Worship Choir. It was hot and I had realized I was having burning pain from little bumps on the inside of my right leg possibly caused from Shingles though I had not had the condition before. After the rehearsal, the choir and orchestra members witnessed on the streets to passersby and invited them to the free concert in the park to take place that night. It was the first time our choir had sung in that type of venue. We had a wonderful praise concert and were thankful as the people attending came forward for counseling concerning salvation.

Then our director was told that the Mayor had been in the audience and wanted to speak. The Mayor told us he was going to do something a politician was always told not to do. He was going to turn his back on the audience because he came on stage to speak to the choir and orchestra. He was a Christian and said when he got off work he liked to walk through the park to see what the citizens in his town were doing. He was so pleased to hear us presenting the Gospel in praise music and thanked us for coming. It was after 9:30 at night when we dispersed to find our places of lodging. I had concerns about trying to locate the parking lot where I had left my van since it was so dark. The lot was distinctive in that it was not paved, there was no attendant and payment had to be made with one dollar bills stuffed in a section of the metal boxes with numbers that corresponded with the parking space. I walked several blocks, but could not find the parking lot.

I passed several other lots and decided to check my new I-Phone with the application "Find My Car." The application showed me the location, but no street names so it was of little help. I stopped in a pizza shop and described the parking lot, but none of the employees seemed to know where it was. I walked a few more blocks and asked the Lord to send me a policeman who could help me. When I had walked about a half block, two policemen came around the corner walking toward me.

I stopped them by saying, "God sent you. I am from out of town and don't know this area. I just prayed for a policeman to help me find the parking lot where I left my van."

I gave the description of the parking lot and they gave me some general directions which did not help me find my van, but I was getting closer. A lady who was attending a parking lot near me saw my need, came across the street, and when I described the place I left the van, told me how to find it. After walking three blocks I found the dim lit area and thanked the Lord for all the people He put in my path to help me. Needless to say, I was very pleased to find my van, locate the motel a few miles away and get settled for the night.

In all these things, He directed me and kept me safe.

Ask Yourself...

When I feel weak, do I turn the situation over to my loving heavenly Father knowing when I am weak, He is strong?

Record in your journal how God has given you strength to face tough situations in your life. Be prepared to share these times with others who need to hear of His great love for them.

Read 2 Corinthians 12:10.

What is God's promise to you concerning His great love when you are feeling weak?

How has this section changed the way you pray for your needs in the face of circumstances requiring spiritual strength?

We continue "leaning on the everlasting arms, safe and secure from all alarms" as the hymn says so well and encourage you to do the same. He is faithful and cares for you. He will supply all your needs in Christ Jesus. Just ask and believe, seek, knock, and He will come to you and meet your needs. To Him who is able to bring it to pass, we give all the praise!

PART FIFTEEN
FINANCIAL MIRACLES

-137-

PROBLEMS WITH THE VAN

O ne Friday morning when we got in the van to go to town, the L.E.D read-out showed that our van was due for the 3,000-mile checkup, but the sticker on the windshield showed we had another 1,000 miles before service was due. On the day we had planned to take the van in for service, I tried to crank the van and it hesitated and made a strange noise. I tried again and it cranked. I began to think that must have been the reason the indicator showed it was time for service. I told the man on duty about the strange indicator and that we were not due for service for another 1,000 miles. He said the mechanic would check it out with the other general checkpoints to be considered. When the mechanic at the Chrysler dealership tried to move the van, he had a hard time cranking it also. After the repairs were made, the mechanic asked me if I'd had the same problem and how long had it been going on. I told him just that morning and God must have had us check the indicator, so we could get the service needed that day, even when we did not know there was be a problem.

**What a wonderful God to show us these things,
the large and the small, for our good.**

13 8 —

ROOT CANAL

A week before the van problem, I had pain in one of my teeth and called my dentist. She was on vacation, so I left a message on her voice mail telling her about the tooth. She called me and told me to come see her when she got back to work on July 13. On her first day back at work after the vacation she told me to come into her office so she could exam the tooth. After the van was repaired and a new battery put in, I went to have my check-up. I was sure I needed to have a root canal, but the dentist did not think so from what I had told her. At the appointment, she took an X-ray of the tooth and told me that indeed I did need a root canal. After having a root canal in 2006, I was not ready to have another one, but it was needed. When I called to make the appointment with Dr. Van Carroll in Dothan, I realized that the Lord had already given us the moneys a week before through a $1,000 refund from the IRS with a letter stating we had been charged too much on our 2008 taxes!

-139-

AFFORDABLE MEDICATION

The third week in July of 2009, I called in a request for a prescription to Paramore's Pharmacy for David's Oxycontin which was not covered by Covenant Hospice. David was concerned because he knew the last time he had picked up the prescription for Oxycontin at 20 mg the cost was $290.00. When the Pharmacist checked on her supply of Oxycontin, she told us she was sorry but she did not have the 20 mg. Then she asked if we would agree to have her fill the prescription with the 40 mg tablets since David was supposed to take two tablets of 20 mg three times a day. The total Oxycontin dose would be the same: two 20 mg or one 40 mg every 8 hours. We asked how much that bottle of medication would be.

She said, "$15.00."

God worked out the situation and saved us $275.00. We did not even know the medicine came in 40 mg.

**Our Father watches over us and cares about
all these matters. It is so evident to us.**

-140-

JERRY'S ELEVENTH-HOUR MIRACLE JOB

Michele, Jerry, and their three children (ages seventeen, fourteen, and twelve) moved back to Jacksonville, Florida, on June 18, 2009, to seek employment in the Duval County School System. Jerry's job was cut in the Marion County School System where he had taught sixth grade Science for a year due to the economic downturn. Even with Michele's earnings from her job in the school system working as a paraprofessional they did not have enough income to meet their needs. He and the family had lived in Jacksonville, his home town for about eleven years prior to his being called to preach. He was in a little church-start and did not have enough income to provide for the family, so after prayer and seeking the Lord's will, he was led to get a job teaching in the school system. He and Michele had prayed about the job cut and felt God leading them back to Jacksonville to find jobs.

They moved into a home left to Jerry in his maternal grandparents' will, so they had no house payment in Jacksonville. They planned to rent out the house they built in Anthony so they could make the monthly payments on their mortgage. Each of them applied for jobs online in the Duvall County School System but found no job openings. Jerry requested a face-to-face interview with a school board official to follow through with his attempt to be employed as a teacher.

On Monday, August 10, 2009, Jerry took fourteen-year-old Kyle to Sandalwood High School and filled out paperwork for his

329

enrollment for the school year. As they were leaving the school they noticed a teacher, moving some heavy boxes of material and offered to help her. She was delighted that they offered to help and told them she had several other items to move if they had the time to assist her. They were more than glad to help. Jerry jokingly asked her when their school was going to hire some teachers and that he needed a job. They talked a few minutes and each realized the other was a Christian. The teacher told him she would call her friend who was the principal at Ed White High School to see if she might have a job opening. When she called her friend she was told to send Jerry over for an interview. He went to Ed White High School, had the interview with the lady who also was a Christian, and was hired to teach ninth grade Science! The interviewer told Jerry she would love to have another Christian on her staff.

**God continues to provide for His own,
even at the eleventh hour.**

Jerry was told report to work Tuesday, August 11, the very next day! How great is our God and how He loves to provide! What a wonderful answer to prayer that was! Michele was to have an interview the next day at an ESE school. She was concerned because she had worked with autistic children in a classroom in Anthony and had a lot of problems with her back as a result of having to lift some of the larger children. She knew she could not do that same kind of work, but was willing to have the interview and see what God worked out for her.

-141-

MICHELE'S JOB

On August 9, 2010, Michele called to ask us to pray for her as she went to a job interview with a school principal in Jacksonville, Florida. For weeks she had sent out resumes, looking for a job as a paraprofessional, a job she had done in the Anthony, FL area for six years and in Jacksonville 5 months the past school year. We prayed she would get to work with the children as she had done in Anthony and not just do busy work as she had been asked to do in the Jacksonville school. Jerry asked that we pray she would be hired on the spot in order to have a job when school started the next week. We prayed specifically as they had asked. Michele called back in about three hours to tell us that the interview went well and that she was hired on the spot. She was told she would get to work with third-grade students who needed a little extra help.

God answered in a wonderful way to strengthen the faith of all who were asked to pray. How He loves to pour out these blessings on His children!

-142-

DENTAL AND HOUSEHOLD EXPENSE MET

During August of 2009, we had unexpected expenses. On our fixed income of Social Security and Retirement, we were in need of yet another miracle to meet these needs. Woodrats had come into our basement and damaged the insulation. The air conditioner units had not been working properly. A new motor had to be installed and other repairs were necessary.

In July, I had to have a root canal and the bill was due in August. Eighteen days after the root canal, as I was eating breakfast, my bridge composed of three teeth fell out in my oatmeal. Wouldn't you know it, the tooth where the expensive root canal had been done was a part of the bridge! This occurred on Friday. Our dentist did not open her office on Fridays but was very conscientious about checking her messages on her answer phone, in case of emergencies. I called and left a message concerning the problem. The dentist called back in about fifteen minutes and discussed the situation with me, telling me to come in for an appointment on Monday. The process took two appointments to complete, one week apart. It was time for the 6-month cleaning the week the bridge was re-cemented. That was an extra charge. Again, I asked for a miracle to help us pay the present expenses.

We sold a riding lawn mower for $500.00 and used that money to pay some of the bills. An unexpected check came from a timeshare company in New Hampshire for a percentage of the rental of a property we were trying to sell through the same company.

That gave us another $299.00 toward payment our expenses. On Wednesday, August 25, 2009, I received a call from Jenny, a teacher we had worked with at Malone School in Malone, Florida. She had been re-assigned for the new school year to Riverside Elementary School in Marianna to work with ESE students. The interpreter who had been hired to work with two Deaf boys who were to be in her class had resigned after only three days in the new school year, to take another job. Jenny asked me to work, starting the next day, as a substitute interpreter until a full-time interpreter could be found.

God provided yet again for the extra income we needed.

David and I attended a dinner the next week provided for the members of the local Farm Bureau. After the meal and program, there were door prizes given away. About 350 members were present. Each of us had a ticket with numbers on them. As the drawing of tickets took place, several coffee mugs were given out to those who had the right number. Cans of peanuts and various other small items were presented. The larger prizes were saved until last. A few $25 Farm Bureau memberships were won by ticket holders. The Master of Ceremonies announced that the last presentation would be $100 in cash. I asked the Lord to allow David or me to win the money if that was His will, due to the heavy expenses we had for the month. When the ticket number was read, 575, David sat there wondering if he had heard the number correctly. It was his number! After a few seconds to let it sink in that he had won, he stood and raised his hand. One of the children, who handed out the gifts, brought David the envelope with the $100 inside.

I am sure many people present needed the money, but God was so gracious to give it to David and we were grateful. We praised Him for being so interested in the things that concerned us. We know He is the provider and He cares about the big and small things in life. He answers just for His good pleasure and pours out blessings for every need. We deserve nothing. He provides everything!

A friend from First Baptist Church, Marianna, who was present that night, came over and talked with David and me for about five minutes. We had not seen her for a long time. She told us that she was attending a church in Panama City, but realized she needed to get back to her "home church." Then she mentioned that she had bought several tickets to the "Point of Grace" concert to be held September 25 in the Panama City church where she attended. I was aware of the event and had it written on my home calendar, not expecting to attend, but having it there to remind me to tell others who might be interested in going. The friend told us that she had given two tickets to some good friends of ours and wanted us to have tickets also. She expressed appreciation to David for playing the organ at her family weddings and all we had meant to her and to our church. This was her way of saying "thank you."

We left the meeting humbled by God's unexpected blessings,giving thanks to the One from whom all blessings flow.

-143-

IRS MAKES ANOTHER ERROR

David began taking Nexavar chemo pills on November 14, 2009. I had been thinking about the fact we could use another $1,000 and asked the Lord to take care our needs as He saw fit. The same month, we received yet another refund from IRS stating they had made an error and owed us another $1,000 plus.

Miracle of miracles, the IRS made a mistake, acknowledge the fact and was giving us a second refund in nine months after we paid the money they said we owed back in the spring of 2009!

This was enough to take care of the Periodontist treatment. Dr. Pittman in Dothan planned to put in an implant as soon as I had the money to cover the expense. My appointment with Dr. Pittman was set for December 1, 2009. I was told I would need to have X-rays taken to see if the bone graft done in August had produced enough bone to enable the dentist to put in the implant. I prayed about having enough money to take care of the additional X-rays and for the Lord to show me what was best. After the X-rays were read by the dentist, he told me there was not enough bone to do the procedures. The Lord showed me that it was best not to have the implant and there was no need to spend the money. When I was leaving the office, I asked what the charges were for the X-rays and was told there was no charge and that the X-rays were included in the total cost of the periodontal treatment. I was amazed I was leaving the office without any charges for services rendered!

-144-

THE MONITOR

The last week of July 2010, my monitor for the computer died while I was typing an email message to a friend. I turned off the computer that night and tried to get my monitor to come on the next day. It would only flash about every three seconds. I called my friend, Mark, who is certified in Microsoft, to get his opinion from what I described. We both agreed from what I had tried and the results that the problem was the monitor.

I did not have a sitter lined up to be with David, so I decided to call a friend who was well versed in computers and ask him if he could pick up a monitor for me. I left a voice mail for him at work and in a few minutes, he called me back. He told me he was not working with computers much at that time, but his son who was in the local college could take care of the situation for me when he got out of class that afternoon. What I had prayed during this time was that someone would come to the house, check the computer and monitor to make sure what I needed, and set up the new monitor for me.

In the meantime, I called the computer store and talked with Joe, the tech my friend Kay recommended, telling him I had decided to buy the 19" monitor and would have a college student pick it up for me around 4 P.M. when he got out of class since it would be hard for me to come and leave David alone. Joe was concerned about selling me a monitor unless I was sure that was what I needed. He asked where I lived and realized my home was about a mile from his business. It was as though God touched his heart.

Although I knew they did not make house calls to check out computer equipment, he said, "You said you lived close to our store. I think I will send Nick out to check your computer and monitor. I will send the monitor with him so he can install it for you. Then we can write up a ticket on your charge when we are sure it is a monitor you need."

I thanked him and told him that was an answer to prayer, and it was another little miracle I had asked for.

This was not a matter of any eternal consequence, but just for God's good pleasure, I had asked Him to take care of this matter for me.

Nick talked with me by phone, got directions to our house, and said he was familiar with the area. He came within ten minutes, checked out the equipment, and installed the new large screen monitor. How blessed I was in a matter of about two hours, all was taken care of and I was back online!

I called Joe and gave him the credit card information for my bill and thanked him again for all his help. The college student called about the time Nick left, so I was able to share the testimony with him. I called his daddy to let him know what God had done for me and that I no longer needed their help. Then I sent a few emails out to share the testimony of God's provisions for me.

-145-

FINGERPRINTS AND THE PUBLISHER

Every five years, the Jackson County School Board required that part-time employees, such as substitute interpreters for the Deaf, be fingerprinted and sign a form stating his or her interest in working for the school year at hand. When I received my letter from the JCSB in July 2010, I signed the form, took it by the school board office, and went to the UPS store where I was to be fingerprinted. The day after the prints were made, I was called by a lady from the JCSB and told the fingerprints were not acceptable and therefore I would have to go back to the UPS office and have them taken again.

The next day, I returned to the UPS office and the same lady who had taken the prints the day before took me to the back of the store to try once again to get an acceptable set of prints. As she was talking to a friend who worked in a UPS store in a town nearby, there was mention of the busy life they both had. Judy, the lady who was taking my prints, mentioned that one of her jobs was a publisher. That caught my attention because of the book I continue to write, "Miracles in My Life" or "Testimonies of God's Miracles," a sub-title that I keep in mind so as to be careful to give God the credit for the miracles He sends. I mentioned the book to her and the fact I wrote poetry. She was not aware until I told her, that there was another publisher in Marianna, just a few blocks from her business. I had talked with the other lady years before after hearing about her from her pastor. She had been very encouraging and was interested in printing the type of book that I was writing. At that time, the cost would have been prohibitive. It is interesting that

God worked out the miracle of introducing me to a publisher who "just happened" to be taking my prints the day she told her friend that she was a publisher. Had my prints not been turned down by the school board the first time, I would not have known that there was a way to have my book published at a reasonable price, and possibly be used of the Lord in some mighty way. I began sending her questions about printing my book and she was gracious enough to answer my email inquiries.

-146-

CONFERENCE FEES

David and I attended the Joy Club meeting in August at our local Baptist church. The pastor made an announcement concerning a trip being planned for the members of the group for Celebrators week with nationally known Christian speaker, David Jeremiah, October 17-22 in Sevierville, TN. The music was to be led by a well-known Christian vocalist, Charles Billingsley, son of Clyde and Judy, former seminary classmates of David's and mine. A well-known Christian quartet was to be featured on one of the night sessions.

When David heard the announcement, he told me that he wanted us to go. That particular day, he felt very bad and was sitting in his wheelchair for the meeting and meal. The pastor asked that those of us who were interested in going to raise our hands. As the members raised their hands, it appeared to be enough people to make it worth-while to charter a bus, make motel reservations, and attend the conference. The pastor handed out a form indicating the total cost for the round trip with an itinerary of the daily conference events. The charge was $125.00 each.

A few days later, David received a letter with a check from Medicare for the amount of $250.00. I opened the letter and read it to David due to the fact he had an eye infection and was having trouble seeing clearly. I asked what he would like to do with the money.

He said, "Let's put it toward our trip to Tennessee."

I asked him if he realized that the amount for the conference fee was $250.00, the same amount of the check!

It looked as though the Lord was showing us
He was going to see that we did get to go to the conference.

-147-

CREDIT UNION

After David's home-going, Christy, Michael, and the boys wanted me to stay a few days with them. However, I felt it was best for me to return home and start taking care of the business at hand, settling the estate as best I could. I had called Jayme Alfano, representative of Mass Mutual Insurance Company to let him know of the death on December 27. He started the process of getting paperwork sent by email for me to fill out and return to him. I contacted Farm Bureau, Wells Fargo bank, the County Tax Collector, the local college that had insurance set aside for David as interpreter for the Deaf, and other agencies that needed certified death certificates. The Lord worked all things together for good and gave me continued peace to deal with all the business.

The day I went to the local credit union to close out a special checking and savings account David had set up and the lockbox in our name, I spoke with a bank officer who took care of the transactions for me. I showed her the checkbook and told her the balance was $171.00 according to my records. I told her when I went online to check the credit union records, I found the institution showed that we had more money in the account that we actually had. That was a good "problem," but very confusing.

She brought up our account in her computer and told me the bank owed us $400.00. That was a miracle of God and I let her know it was. I asked her to check my figures against the computer figures to make sure of the amount due to me. She looked at the checkbook entries and compared them to the bank figures. They matched, but she said the amount due was $400.00. Who was I to disagree with records of a financial institution? She paid me the $400.00.

After I surrendered the keys to the lockbox and put the contents of the box in an envelope provided by the credit union representative, I reminded her once again that the Lord had performed another miracle for me. He knew that I would no longer get my Social Security payments each month starting in February 2011 and that my income would be about $534.00 less per month. I had thought about that and wondered how the Lord would make up the difference.

**I knew He would work it out and get the credit
for all the blessings He sent.**

The $400.00 was just the beginning of what He had in store for me! A few weeks later, I was asked by the credit union representative to come by and sign a form so I could get the balance in the Savings account. When I had signed the paper, the representative gave me a check for $106.88. I was aware the total of money paid to me from the credit union was $506.88, within a few dollars of the $534.00 I had previously been getting in my Social Security check. One of my friends from my hometown who had attended the graveside service for David sent me a check about a week later for $200.00. My aunt from Savannah sent me $100.00 the same week. This was $172.00 more than I would normally have received that month. God not only made up the difference in the amount that would be lost in February but gave me more than I could have expected.

As the song says, "He giveth and giveth and giveth again."

-148-

Debt Free

On February 11, 2011, about six weeks after David's home-going, all the financial matters were settled with Mass Mutual. The money in the annuity we had set aside for David's Long Term Care was not used for his medical expenses since he was under hospice care a year and half before his death. Therefore, the annuity was closed out when David died, then established in my name. A check for David's Life Insurance was sent to me after the necessary paperwork was sent to our insurance representative in Jacksonville, while other papers were sent to Mass Mutual's home office. At that time, the Lord helped me pay off a bank loan and the funeral expenses. Once again, I was debt free! Our home in Marianna had been paid off in eight years in 2004. The loan for the mountain house David wanted us to buy in 2005 was paid off in five years. Only a miracle of God could have brought all this to pass.

God has blessed abundantly just for His good pleasure and trusted me with gifts from His hand.

-149-

THE CHECK IN THE MAIL

As I walked out to my front yard, and as I often do when going to get the mail, spoke to the Lord and asked, "Lord, do you have some exciting mail for me today or maybe a check?" I opened the box and pulled out the mail. There were two or three agencies sending a request for donations, a sales paper, and a personal card from an interpreter for the Deaf who lived in a town nearby. I assumed she had heard about David's death and was sending me a sympathy note. As I opened the card, I realized there was a check inside. When I got inside the house, I sat down to see if the lady had sent a donation for Gideon Bibles or Covenant Hospice, the two memorials we had set up in David's memory. The note informed me that she and her husband wanted to pay the balance on a car they bought from us in 2004. I unfolded the check and to my amazement, I saw the amount of $1,000.00! I sat very still for a moment and could hear in my mind the conversation I had just had that same morning with the timeshare salesperson, "Even if I had $1,000.00 in my hand I would not send you the money."

I thanked the Lord, for this miracle. It was amazing to me because David had kept the records of the sale of the car and had not mentioned it to me when the payments came in. I checked his laptop computer and could not find any record of the monthly payment schedule nor when they were received. He had not mentioned the vehicle in years. If someone had asked me if the lady and her husband had paid for the car, I would have assumed they had since so much time had passed. Then I realized the amount of the check was about one third the amount I needed for our double bronze grave markers. I told the Lord I could see how He was working out the payment for the markers and praised Him again for His provision.

The next day, I went to the mailbox to check the mail and remembered the exciting events of the previous day, smiled, and opened the box to see what surprises I might find. There was a check from a settlement from a general lawsuit due to something I had ordered in the mail. I assumed it was for a dollar or two, as I have noticed these things usually are, but the check was for $43.79. I could only smile and say, "Thank you, Lord, for the $43.79 I can add to my $1,000.00 toward the purchase of the marker."

The next day I went to the mailbox and my payment for interpreting at the college from the month before was in the box. It was not a large amount, but that $40.00 was added to the other two checks to be held until the rest of the money was secured. That walk to the mailbox has become exciting each day, an adventure as I anticipate what blessing the Lord is sending. Sometimes it is a letter from a lady I met in England while at the International Church Music Conference in Coventry, England. It is rare to hear from her, but I send her Christmas cards and now and then she will write me a letter.

**Sometimes, the Lord sends a check and usually,
it is just in time to pay a bill
or take care of some necessity, but it is always an
adventure of faith.**

-150-

Hip Replacement

In June of 2012, two years after my fall from the choir loft at Idlewild Baptist Church, I called to schedule my right hip replacement surgery by Dr. Brodersen, Head of Orthopedic Surgery at Mayo Clinic in Jacksonville. He was the surgeon who did my left knee replacement in 2005 and I preferred him doing the hip surgery. Both my children lived in the Jacksonville area, so it was more convenient for all of us for me to have the surgery done there. I called Mayo Clinic after praying about the insurance situation and asked if my new insurance coverage from Aetna All-in-One Plan would be accepted. The representative with whom I spoke told me the institution did not accept the plan.

I prayed about finding another surgeon in the Jacksonville area. Family and friends who had surgery in Jacksonville gave me names of doctors they would recommend. I called two of the doctors who were suggested, one who did surgery at Beaches Hospital and the other at Memorial Hospital. Both told me the coverage would be accepted, but one was "out of network" and would cost more for the procedure. The other was "in network" and would cost less.

After setting up an appointment with the hospital and doctor who was "in network," I prayed again and asked the Lord to work a miracle so that my insurance would be accepted by Mayo Clinic and I could have the surgery done by Dr. Brodersen. When I called Mayo Clinic for the second time, the scheduling department representative told me that Mayo Clinic had just started accepting Aetna's All-in-One-Plan, but only if it was a PPO. My insurance plan "just happened to be" a PPO plan! The lady I spoke with set up a date for pre-op and surgery. It was exciting to see how God had turned the tide once again to bless me in such a personal way.

When the week for pre-op arrived, I drove to Jacksonville to stay with my daughter, Michele. I went to my appointment, filled out the necessary papers, and had blood work done. On the day of surgery, I got up early and my daughter and her family took me to the new hospital section of the Davis Building. My daughter's Minister of Music from Kernan Blvd. Baptist Church met us there, as well my son, Michael, and grandson from South Georgia. I was taken back to the surgical area and prepared for surgery.

As I was being asked questions and being checked out for the last time prior to surgery, I mentioned to one of the young doctors that I'd had Shingles a few months before and some scaring was left behind. The doctor looked at the little scars on the inside of my right leg and was very concerned about whether the surgery could take place. I had been covering the area with a Band-aid a few days before and the area appeared to be a bit "weepy." The doctor consulted with my surgeon and soon returned to let me know the surgery could not be done due to a possibility of infection. He suggested I call the hospital in a month to reschedule the surgery. I was disappointed and knew the family would be, too, but I understood the surgical team was being cautious and appreciated their lofty standards. After all, Mayo Clinic has a great reputation and the way my situation was handled is one reason why.

In July, I called Mayo Clinic and set up appointments for pre-op and surgery. Pre-op was scheduled for July 17. I stayed with my daughter and her family in Jacksonville until the day of surgery, July 24. We arrived about 7 a.m. at the Mayo surgical area, as we had done in June. This time everything went like clockwork! The surgery took about two hours, but I had to wait in the surgical area until about an hour afterward until a patient room was ready. My family was not told why it was taking so long. Some of them had to leave the hospital to go back to work. Michele was the only one who remained until the hospital staff brought me to my room.

I was pleased she had come prepared to stay two nights with me to make sure I had any assistance I might need. My physical therapy started the next day. I did well, though I was weak. In fact, the therapist and the nurses said I was doing better than the twenty-year-old men on that floor of the hospital. They said those guys were their worst patients. My insurance covered four days in the hospital, so I was given the names of several facilities where I could choose to go for my rehabilitation on the fourth day. I chose Brooks Rehabilitation Center at St. Luke's Hospital which was also a part of St. Vincent's Hospital.

On July 27, I was taken to the rehab hospital by EMS. My son came that day to take my suitcase and personal items to Brooks. He followed the transport vehicle in his car and stayed with me a while to make sure I had everything I needed before he went back home. The next day, I met the Brooks doctor who was assigned to my case. He informed me that my insurance would pay for six days in rehab. I was amazed since I could not walk at the time! I told the doctor we had our work cut out for us.

The rehab exercises went well each day and on day six, I was released. My son came to get me checked out and took me to his home in Georgia, about forty miles north of Jacksonville. A few days later, after the paperwork was faxed to me, filled out, and returned to doctors and the insurance company, I started therapy at Advanced Rehabilitation a few miles away. I went three times a week for two weeks and the last week I was told I was doing well enough to drop the last day of therapy, perhaps due to the many activities I took part in with my son's family.

During the three weeks, I was in South Georgia, I went to eight football games to see one of my grandsons play in his eighth-grade games, the other grandson play in his ninth-grade games, and I attended the varsity games, rain or shine. The family had their house on the market for sale and also had appointments with a realtor to look at homes they might be interested in buying. Therefore, we were out and about, climbing stairs, and walking a good bit, so I had some extra exercise during those three weeks to add to the therapy I had at the rehab center!

Their house had been on the market for about a year at this point. It was shown twice by the realtor while I was in town. One Sunday as we left the house for lunch during the second showing, I told them I was praying that the couple who looked at the house that day would like the house and its special features so well they would make an offer, the sellers could make a counteroffer, and the house would sell. The realtor called my son and his wife the next day to tell them the couple had made an offer. They made a counter offer and the house was sold! How exciting it was to be a part of this special blessing of answered prayer! On September 2, my son and his family brought me back to Marianna. Six weeks after surgery, I was allowed to start driving, take care of my daily duties, and was back to living alone, just Jesus and me.

-151-

THE FWCO WORSHIP PROJECT IN NYC, MAY 31-JUNE 4, 2014

After two years of praying and planning, approximately 354 members of the Florida Worship Choir and Orchestra and a few family members flew from nine airports on May 31, 2014, to minister in the New York City area. Upon arrival, the group of 200 or so was transported by bus with our tour directors from Celebration Choir Tours, to Central Park for rehearsal and presentation of the choir's 2014 repertoire. Crowds gathered to hear the group with great enthusiasm! Vendors were in the park selling refreshments, weddings were taking place near the fountain by the lake, and tumblers were performing feats with some volunteer participation from the passersby for their entertainment.

Rain had been predicted for the day, but the Lord held it off until we sang our last song. Then the sprinkles came down as we walked seven blocks to meet the tour buses that took us to the Crowne Plaza Hotel, our home away from home. Saturday was a free day to sightsee and rest a bit. Sunday morning, June 1, the groups to which we had been assigned prior to departure on the trip, boarded tour buses and departed to leading church services in eleven new church-starts, established by the North American Mission Board, Atlanta, Georgia. The group to which my daughter, granddaughter, and I were assigned with seven other musicians, ministered to a small congregation of people from India on Sunday night. It was amazing how God worked out the money for our three-generations to be a part of such a great ministry opportunity!

Our group of ten took the Staten Island Ferry to New Jersey, passing famous landmarks like the Statue of Liberty and the Brooklyn Bridge. We walked for miles to see the memorial at Ground Zero where the Twin Towers were destroyed, and road the double-decker Gray Line Bus back to the Crowne Plaza Hotel for a little rest. The groups of musicians who took part in the Sunday morning services did a Flash Mob of worship music Sunday night in Times Square, which was put on YouTube for the world to see for all posterity!

On Monday, June 2, the entire group was taken from the Crown Plaza by bus to get assigned positions on stage at the beautiful world-famous Carnegie Hall in preparation for the worship concert that night. We had an hour break to find a place to eat from the many choices of restaurants near the Hall and return an hour before the concert. A large group attended that night and the place was filled with worship!

We travel to Brooklyn, on Tuesday, June 3, to be a part of the Prayer Service at Brooklyn Tabernacle. There was no place for our orchestra on stage, so many of the instrumentalists sang with us in the large choir loft. Prior to the service, we met Reverend and Mrs. Jim Cymbala, leaders of the church. We then walked across the street for a box supper and returned for the three-hour prayer service. There was an hour of silent prayer, an hour for special prayer needs including prayer for prisoners who had written the pastor asking for prayer for their families, and prayer for a mission team from the church who was going to Uganda to do mission work. Our choir had the opportunity of singing two of the praise songs and then asked to sing one more at the close of the service. The large church with three balconies was filled with worshippers and a sweet spirit was in that place.

As we traveled home on June 4, we were aware of God having worked in mighty ways to allow us to sing His praise and "push back the darkness" during the two years of preparation and planning. Our leaders were told there was little chance that we could present the musical in the various venues, yet God turned the hearts of the city officials and others in prominent positions. Opposition and prohibitions were changed to "permission granted." God opened every door!

We were kept safe in His care through our travels and given freedom to spread His Word to thousands of people from all over the world going to and fro in that great city!

Ask Yourself...

Am I now aware how much God cares about the big and small things in my life?

Will I commit to worship Him and daily thank Him for His great mercy, grace, and love?

Record in your journal how worshipping God has changed your life. Ask Him to guide you to those who need to hear what you have learned about God's amazing love!

Read Psalm 100.

Make Psalm 150 your personal commitment to praise Him!

-152-

HURRICANE MICHAEL

On October 9, 2018, I drove to Blairsville, Georgia to spend a few weeks in the area and enjoyed our mountain house. All along my trip, I would check the weather radar app on my cell phone keeping up with the hurricane headed toward the Florida Panhandle. It appeared to be turning to the east between Marianna and Tallahassee which meant Marianna would probably get heavy rain and wind but not a lot of damage. The people in that area heard on the late news that the storm was downgraded to a category one with a wind speed of 75 miles per hour. During the wee hours of October 10, the storm excelled to a category four or in some areas a category five, between 140 mph and 150 mph, the strongest hurricane to ever hit the U.S! The landscape was forever changed in a matter of minutes! Many houses were completely destroyed. Businesses were damaged or destroyed and most of the trees were down or left broken, looking like sticks standing in the mud from all the water that accumulated during days of rain. Crops were destroyed. Animals were killed, but there was no loss of human life by the grace of God! A week later a young man was killed when he went out to clean up some limbs on his property. A tree fell on him and he died.

One of my Florida neighbors called to let me know a tree had fallen on my house. My house was surrounded by a tree belt. Through the years, we had taken town six pine trees that were damaged by lightning during summer storms. I had just paid to have several trees near the house taken down a week before the hurricane, planning to have others in the front tree bed taken down when I received my next retirement check.

Michael came from North Carolina to see about the damage to my house. He and his wife had a job transfer on September 1 to New Bern, North Carolina, and had just gone through Hurricane Florence on September 12. Through the grace of God, they had no damage to their home, though others on their street were under water. When he arrived at my house, he realized not one tree, but many large trees had fallen on the roof and water was damaging the South side of the house where the master bedroom, closet, laundry room, and garage were located. The water accumulated in the ceiling and spread to other parts of the house as well as soaking the carpets. He and I communicated by phone and text to try and find someone with a crane to remove the trees. After a week of it raining in my bedroom, his sister-in-law in South Georgia contacted a crane and tree removal service and they came down and removed the huge trees adding a tarp to secure the roof. Michael turned in their bill for services to the local FL Farm Bureau office for payment. He stood in line with many distraught victims of the catastrophe as they sought help from the insurance company. Many did not know what to do next. Adjusters from several states were called in to help the thousands of citizens that needed to have their home and property assessed to see how much coverage they could receive. Michael was given a check for $17,700.00 which he brought to me in Ellijay, Georgia on his way back to North Carolina. I had the bank in Blairsville wire the money to my Wells Fargo account in Marianna and then wrote a check to the crane and tree service in South Georgia thanking them for all their help.

When the next rain came a week later, the blue tarps came up on one end and it rained again in my bedroom until we could find someone to secure the tarp. A local man and his helper from Ocala put the tarp back in place for me. We had more rain a few days later and when I checked the house, the wind had blown another small area of the tarp up on one end and I watched it rain even more on the bedroom carpet that bulged up from the wet particle board underneath. The third time the tarp was secured, there was no more water coming in. I felt that was progress. The contractor came over to assess the damages and the adjuster sent me an email word file itemizing the damages he found of $144,114.00. After deductible of almost $6,000.00, the FL Farm Bureau sent me a check for $138,166.00 toward the renovation of the house. I sent that information to the contractor so he and the adjuster could communicate the needs at that point. All things were working together for the restoration and I had perfect peace knowing God was taking care of it all and leading me to the right people to do the work.

The only place I could find to stay close to Marianna on October 28 when I returned to Florida, was in Tallahassee near Interstate 10. When I was 100 miles from Tallahassee, I began to see blue tarps on houses and barns and hundreds of trees downed or damaged! I prayed about a place to stay and the Lord whispered "Microtel" in my spirit. I knew He was saying I was to stay in the Microtel Motel in Marianna. After one night in Tallahassee, I left the next day to drive to Marianna. There was so much damaged on the way to Marianna. The familiar scenes along the interstate appeared to be places I had never been before. Highway signs were down or destroyed for the most part. When I arrived in Marianna, I went to a motel across from the Microtel to see if they had rooms available. Their rooms were all occupied and had been since the storm. I went to the Microtel and saw signs "Do not enter" posted on the lobby door. A man from FEMA was going in the lobby as I stood reading the sign. I asked him if I could go in and he said it was fine. When I talked with the motel clerk she said they did not have any rooms ready. They had no roof damage, but the wind and rain had drenched the rooms so nothing was ready for occupancy. I told the clerk that the Lord has told me "Microtel" so I was sure I was to stay there. She wrote down my name and cell phone number and said as soon as a room was cleaned and ready, she would call me. I went to my regularly scheduled monthly chiropractic appointment and while I was there, the clerk called to say my room was ready. God had provided yet again. The room did not have phone service restored at that point, nor TV, nor AC, but I had lights, water, clean towels, a microwave, a small refrigerator, and a washer and dryer was on the same floor where I was staying. I had my personal items with me that I had packed in my suitcase and used on my trip in the mountains. So, all my basic needs were met.

Each day that week, I went across the highway and bought food items from Walmart or ate at Ruby Tuesdays or the Subway close by. One night, a couple from my church saw me as I went in Walmart and they were on their way out. We exchanged stories of our experience relating to the storm and we went our separate ways. When the couple arrived home, the lady of the house was concerned about me staying in the motel and suggested to her husband that they ask me to come stay in their garage apartment that was attached to their home. I moved in on November 3 and continued to stay there while my home was being repaired. I had been told that I was #73 or so on my contractor's list. I was content to stay in my lovely new quarters until the Lord provided a more permanent place in my restored home in His perfect time. During these days, I never was without food, water, or lights. All I needed was supplied by my Father.

Ask Yourself...

How have I seen the Lord provide for me during the storms of life?

Record in your journal how God has provided all that is necessary even during the stormy times in your life.

Read Matthew 8:23-27.

Make Matthew 8:27b your verse for today.

-153-

MOUNTAIN HOUSE SALE

After enjoying the mountain house in North Georgia for thirteen years, the expense of owning two houses became a bit of a financial burden for me on my fixed income. My children could no longer use the house for their vacations due to changing events in their lives. God had been leading me to a path of more financial freedom by showing me the need to sell the house. I knew our family would miss having the house available for our use, but it was a wise decision to put it on the market with my realtor friend, Jane Baer, who had handled the sale of the house when we had purchased it.

The house was put on the market November 1, 2018. When I was in Miami with the FL Worship Choir and Orchestra for our four-day mission project, my realtor called to say she had a verbal offer from a couple who wanted to buy the house! She told me the amount they were offering and I gave a counter offer. They responded and we agreed on a price that fit their budget and limited bank loan. I told the Lord I would accept the amount He had for me. The couple was surprised that I accepted their offer as was the realtor. I told her it was not all about the money. She said that was unusual. God had answered my prayer His way and blessed us both. The buyers secured an inspector to check out the house and I agreed to make the necessary upgrades as I dealt with repairmen, realtor, etc. by phone and text since I was in Florida. I had prayed for Christians to buy the house furniture and all. I wanted to sell the house furnished since I did not want to pay to move or store a house full of furniture. God answered my simple prayer. The buyers were Christians and needed a house with furniture!

When I met the buyers, realtor, and banker at the lawyer's office in Blairsville, Georgia on December 14, I gave my testimony of answered prayer concerning the sale of the house. The buyers gave their testimony through tears of joy about their answered prayers for the house with furniture at the price they could afford. The lawyer gave her testimony about being delivered from alcoholism immediately after she turned the matter over to the Lord, and the banker and realtor were agreeing with us as we testified to how good God is to us all and shared their recent answers to prayer! Through the tears and smiles of joy, the lawyer actually pointed out the areas where we were to sign the necessary papers for the transaction at hand! It was a wonderful time of praise as God had all things work together for our good and His glory!

Ask Yourself...

How has obedience to God led to answered prayers in your life?

Are you willing to give a testimony of God's mercy and grace so that others can be blessed as well?

Record in your journal your testimony and be ready to share it whenever God asks.

Read 2 Timothy 1:8a.

Why should you not be ashamed to testify about our Lord?

-154-

BENEFITS UNEXPECTED

A month after I moved into the garage apartment, my neighbor who had a crew cleaning up trees on his side of the pond on his property, asked me to take care of the tree removal on my side of his pond. His sister was asked to pay for the removal of trees at the head of the body of water on her property. I paid him the amount due to the tree surgeon for my part. At that point that was the only money out of pocket I had to spend that was not covered by FL Farm Bureau.

A week after I paid my across-the-pond neighbor for tree removal, I received a card in the mail from Woodmen of the World Insurance Company stating if I had more than $10,000 worth of damage to my home, I might qualify for a $1,000 benefit. I had a cancer policy set up for me when my husband was diagnosed with cancer, but I had no idea there were any additional benefits with the policy. I made an appointment to talk with the Woodmen representative and as she checked on my policy, paid premiums, etc., she told me I would be sent a check for $1,000 in the next week or so. She also said Woodmen had a gift for me. I assumed it was a token gift of a box of candy or something along those lines. She gave me a Winn Dixie gift card for $50.00!

I left the office that day with a smile as I thought through the expense I had incurred for the removal of the trees by the pond. I told the Lord I could see what He was doing through the discernment He gave me. He was replacing the money I spent, check by check, gift by gift. GA Farm Bureau sent me a check from my home owner's policy for $194.00 due to the sale of my house.

Direct TV sent me a check for $20.16 a few days later. A week later, the man who owned the pond saw me checking my mail at my house. Without the tree belt, he could see our entire community. He drove over in his golf cart and asked me if I would sell him 10 feet more of my property on my side of the pond. Since my house had been for sale several years, he wanted to buy the land before someone else moved in just in case my house was sold. He paid me the amount he had decided would be sufficient. Can you see a pattern here? The Lord more than repaid the amount I had paid out of pocket and received the payment from the same man for more than I had paid him for the tree removal!

As the hymn says so well, "I stand amazed in the presence of Jesus, the Nazarene and wonder how He could love me, a sinner condemned unclean." I am no longer condemned unclean because He washed me, saved me, and presents me to the Father covered by His mercy as a brand-new creature in Christ!

Ask Yourself...

How do I stand before the Lord?

Do you see how much He loves you?

Record in your journal the many amazing ways the Lord has revealed His amazing love for you.

Make Psalm 150 your praise song today.

Biography and Accomplishments of David McCormick
while servings as Manager of BSBA:

Robert David McCormick accepted Christ as Savior at age 9 and was baptized at Hogan BC in Jacksonville, FL. He was the only child in his Christian family and all were active at Hogan Baptist Church. He was called into the music ministry in the summer of his junior year in high school. He graduated from Norman College in Norman Park, GA with an AA degree in Music in 1962. He earned a BA degree in Music from Shorter College in Rome, GA in 1964. In 1966 he graduated from Southwestern Baptist Theological Seminary in Ft. Worth, TX with an additional music degree.

He served on the summer staff for Youth Music Week at Taccoa Baptist Assembly and at Lake Yale Conference Center where he taught music theory through the years. He has served as Interium Minister of Music at First BC in Marianna, FL on two occasions, Handbell Director, and interium organist at First BC and St. Luke's Episcopal Church in Marianna as well as keeping up his work at BSBA.

David served as Minister of Music and Youth at churches in FL and GA over a period of 16 years prior to being called as manager of Blue Springs Baptist Assembly in Marianna, FL in 1982. In 1992 he was approved by the State Board of Missions, FL Baptist Convention, and named Associate Director of Camps and Assemblies.

During his tenure the Blue Springs Baptist Assembly youth facility was completed and expanded; a mobile home park was acquired and expanded; and the adult facilities were substantially improved. He performed such hands on tasks as assisting his wife in the washing and folding of linens, preparation of hundreds of meals, and with Carolyn's help was in charge of all office jobs, as well as welcoming thousands of guests and campers through his 18 years of service for the Lord at Blue Springs Baptist Assembly, 1982-2001.

David and Carolyn McCormick have tried to exemplify the description found in I Chronicles 9:25, that as "gatekeepers" they were entrusted with the responsibilities for the rooms and treasuries in the house of God.

He sang with the Sons of Jubal in GA and the FL Baptist Singing Men's state groups. October of 2006 he went on a music mission tour with the group, combined with the Singing Women's group, to Malaysia and Australia to spread the Gospel. A growth was found on the outside of his intestine in December 2001. The growth was cancerous. At the time of his operation in January 2002, the doctor said he "got it all" and took out six inches of intestine as a precaution. In 2003 the cancer returned and covered the liver. He continued to be active and take a pill form of chemo called Gleevec as well as several supplements. After his retirement he worked in the Jackson County School system as an interpreter for Deaf students K-12 and Chipola College in Marianna. He and his wife, Carolyn, continued to live in Marianna, FL, about a mile from the Conference Center, two miles off I 10.

Biographical information for Carolyn Owens McCormick:

Carolyn Owens McCormick accepted Christ as Savior at age nine in Pembroke, GA where she was baptized at Pembroke Baptist Church where she, her brother and her parents were active. She was called into Christian service at age 12 at Shellman Bluff Christian Camp in South GA. At age 15 she made a recommitment to Christian service at Ridgecrest Baptist Assembly in NC. This is when she confirmed that she would complete her college and seminary training. The Lord provided a college for her by sending the Vice President of Tift College, Forsyth, GA, to her high school to counsel with those students who felt led into Christian service. Carolyn had prayed someone would come from the school God had chosen for her to attend. She was the only one who met with the College representative.

A work scholarship was provided for Carolyn and she helped her family pay her way through four years at Tift College. Her favorite activities involved basketball, archery, singing in the college choir and ensemble, entertaining by singing and accompanying herself on the ukulele. During her second year at Tift her father took his life. It was hard for her mother to continue paying for her college expenses but Carolyn helped by working and applying her earnings toward her education. She completed her college training in 1959 with a Bachelor of Arts degree majoring in Religious Education and having earned a minor in English. She worked four years after graduation as Recreation Worker with American Red Cross, as Recreation and Counselor at GA Baptist Children's Home in Baxley, GA and as secretary at the Home Mission Board in Atlanta, GA (later named North American Mission Board) before going to Southwestern Baptist Theological Seminary in Ft. Worth, TX where she graduated in 1966 with a Masters Degree in Religious Education. While in her second year of seminary she met David. They were married in 1966 in her hometown and returned to Ft. Worth, TX where they were employed after graduation.

She worked closely beside David in the six churches they served together. They have two children. Michele Savery is married to a pastor and high school science teacher. They have two sons, twenty eight and twenty six. In January 2006 they adopted a daughter who is twenty-four years old. She has a one year old son, Carolyn's only great grandchild. Their son, Michael McCormick, manages properties in GA and North Carolina. He and his wife have two sons, ages twenty-two and twenty-one. The children and grandchildren have all accepted Christ as Savior.

Carolyn was secretary at Blue Springs Baptist Assembly from 1982 until her retirement in 2001. She ran the commercial laundry on site for 14 years. She filled in as a cook when needed, and cleaned rooms when the work load increased. She was on the summer camp faculty for Young Musicians at BSBA several years, as well as serving as Dean of Women and Teacher of Hymnology at Lake Yale Conference Center at Youth Music Camp in addition to working at BSBA.

She sings in the FL Baptist Singing Women, a group where she has been a member for over 25 years. She went with the group to sing at the International Church Music Festival in Bern, Switzerland in 1999, with the FL Baptist Singing Men and Women to Coventry, England in 2002 and to do music missions in Malaysia and Australia with the choir, renamed the Florida Worship Choir, in October of 2006 sponsored by the FL Baptist Convention Church Music Department. She enjoys retirement traveling, singing, writing poetry and writing a book about the miracles God has brought to her life.

Her greatest blessings while working at Blue Springs Baptist Assembly (later named Blue Springs Conference Center) was seeing adults and youth come to know Jesus and getting to pray for so many people who came to the facility 12 months a year. God answered those prayers in amazing ways. She grew up going to

Christian camps in GA and NC. God called her into His service in a special way at two of the camps, at age 12 and age 15. A "camp" setting is a wonderful avenue for issuing one into His presence in an intimate way.